I love to bake!

Tana Ramsay

I love to bake!

Tana Ramsay

Contents

Introduction

When I'm writing recipes the most important thing to me is to keep them simple and real – that's the only way I cook for my family.

For the dishes in this book I major on using ingredients that are both seasonal and easily obtainable – food that you or I can pick up on the way home rather than spend hours hunting around for. Online shopping can lighten the task of keeping stocked up on basic household goods and storecupboard staples, making it easier for you to concentrate on fresh ingredients when you're out food shopping. You can then enjoy the luxury of browsing for fruit and vegetables, choosing what looks best and is in season, then pairing it with meat or fish and potatoes or pasta, and so on. This is my favourite way to shop, and it enables me to put together a good variety of meals, rather than cooking the same ones week in, week out.

Looking at websites that offer seasonal charts and accompanying recipe ideas also helps you to shop and cook with the seasons. You may well discover how to prepare ingredients that you don't usually use, enabling you to introduce into your family's meals vegetables and fruits that your children are not familiar with.

As my four get older and more capable, I delegate household jobs to them – from peeling carrots and potatoes to making a marinade and preparing meat for marinating, ready for me to just cook it up – so that cooking supper becomes partly their responsibility too. I also let them each choose a recipe a week. They then write the shopping list for the meal and give it to me to buy the ingredients, and prepare the dish up to the appropriate point when I finish it off. The aim of this is simply to teach them about taking charge of planning meals and organizing themselves enough to think ahead. The kids love this and it shows them how to take into account what we have already eaten that week and to choose something different, therefore ensuring that we maintain a balanced, varied diet.

In this book there are lots of hearty slow-cooked casseroles and spicy bakes, as well as lighter yet equally tasty brunch, lunch or supper dishes and snacks and recipes for everyday traybakes, cupcakes and cookies. I have, of course, also featured some slightly more indulgent recipes, including the most irresistible chocolate pots imaginable, with gorgeously liquid centres. Then there are some easy but tempting fruit pies and tarts, and plenty of savoury ones too, which can be adapted to each season by including different fruit and vegetables. Many of the dishes can be fully or partially prepared in advance for late night suppers or dinner parties.

You will, I hope, find something here to suit every occasion. All these recipes can be adapted to suit your particular taste and none have to be followed exactly. Quite often meals start off with a plan and then somehow go off track, but they can end up being equally delicious. And that's part of the joy of home cooking – there are no rules!

So just eat well and enjoy your home-cooked food. But above all, if and when you can all sit down together, make sure that mealtimes are fun.

cakes & cupcakes

Coffee, walnut & raisin cake

I've not been a huge fan of coffee cakes in the past, but I was bought one recently as a thank you gesture and it was so delicious that I just had to create my own version. This is the result.

Makes
8–10 slices

For the sponge

175g (6oz) unsalted butter, softened, plus extra for greasing

175g (6oz) caster sugar

3 large free-range eggs, beaten

3 tbsp milk

175g (6oz) self-raising flour

1 tsp baking powder

2 tsp instant coffee granules, dissolved in 1 tbsp boiling water

80g (2¾oz) walnut pieces, chopped into small chunks

60g (2¼oz) raisins

For the topping

150g (5½oz) unsalted butter, softened

300g (10½oz) icing sugar

3–4 tsp instant coffee granules, dissolved in 1 tbsp boiling water

60g (2¼oz) walnut pieces

1. Preheat the oven to 200°C/fan 180°C/gas mark 6. Lightly grease a 22cm (8½in) round 5cm (2in) deep cake tin and line the base with parchment paper.

2. To make the sponge, beat together the butter and sugar using a food mixer with a paddle attachment, or with a wooden spoon in a large mixing bowl, until pale and fluffy. Add the eggs and milk a little at a time, beating after each addition. Sift in the flour and baking powder, and fold in with a large metal spoon, then stir in the dissolved coffee granules. When this is all well mixed, gently fold in the walnut pieces and raisins.

3. Tip the cake mixture into the prepared tin, smooth off the top and bake in the oven for 30–35 minutes. The cake should spring back to the touch of a fingertip and be slightly shrinking away from the edge of the tin. Remove from the oven and leave to cool in the tin for 5 minutes then turn out on to a wire rack.

4. Meanwhile, make the topping. Beat the butter in a mixing bowl until soft, then sift in the icing sugar, add the dissolved coffee granules and beat as hard as you can for as much as 10 minutes, if you can bear it, to make it really light and fluffy.

5. When the sponge is completely cool, remove it from the tin and add the topping. Either smooth it over with a knife or be extravagant and pipe in a fancy style over the top, finishing off with the walnut pieces arranged decoratively all over.

Mango & caramel cake

It's best if the mango you use for this cake is still a little firm. The caramel coats it beautifully and makes a gorgeously sticky sauce.

Serves 8

For the topping
100g (3½oz) caster sugar
1 large mango (depending on size and amount of flesh)

For the sponge
175g (6oz) unsalted butter, softened, plus extra for greasing
175g (6oz) caster sugar
3 large free-range eggs, beaten
225g (8oz) plain flour, sifted
1 tsp baking powder
75ml (2½fl oz) milk

1. Preheat the oven to 200°C/fan 180°C/gas mark 6. Lightly grease a 20cm (8in) round cake tin and line the base with parchment paper.

2. Start by making the topping. Put the sugar in an even layer in a small, heavy-based saucepan and heat gently, without stirring, until it begins to melt around the edge. Continue to cook the sugar until it all turns brown, swirling the pan so it caramelizes evenly and no bits start to burn.

3. Quickly tip the caramel into the greased base of the cake tin and tilt the tin to ensure that it evenly coats the base. Leave to cool.

4. Meanwhile, peel the mango, then slice off the two sides as close to the thin stone in the centre as you can. Slice the flesh about 5mm (¼in) thick – you will never get perfectly neat slices and it doesn't matter if you have smaller ones. Arrange the mango slices on top of the caramel, which will have hardened.

5. Now make the sponge. Beat together the butter and sugar using a food mixer with a paddle attachment, or with a wooden spoon in a large mixing bowl, until pale and fluffy. Add the eggs a little at a time, beating after each addition. Fold in the flour and baking powder with a large metal spoon, then stir in the milk, mixing until you have a smooth consistency. Spoon the sponge mixture over the mango in an even layer.

6. Place the tin on a baking sheet and bake in the oven for 50 minutes–1 hour, or until a skewer inserted into the centre comes out clean. Remove from the oven and leave the cake to cool in the tin for 5 minutes, then turn out on to a wire rack.

vanilla sponge birthday cake

Keep this staple recipe on hand for whenever a birthday celebration comes around. You can simply adapt the filling, frosting and decoration however you like to suit the birthday girl or boy and their guests, to make this deliciously light sponge your own.

Serves 8

200g (7oz) unsalted butter, softened, plus extra for greasing
200g (7oz) caster sugar
3 large free-range eggs, beaten
1½ tsp vanilla extract
200g (7oz) self-raising flour, sifted
2 tbsp milk
sweets (such as jelly diamonds or jelly beans) or chocolates (such as crushed chocolate-coated honeycomb balls, crumbled chocolate flake or chocolate buttons) of your choice, to decorate

For the buttercream and filling
150g (5½oz) unsalted butter, softened
150g (5½oz) icing sugar, sifted
few drops of vanilla extract
3 tbsp raspberry jam

1. Preheat the oven to 200°C/fan 180°C/gas mark 6. Lightly grease two 20cm (8in) sandwich tins and line their bases with parchment paper.

2. Beat together the butter and sugar using a food mixer with a paddle attachment, or with a wooden spoon in a large mixing bowl, until pale and fluffy. Add the eggs a little at a time, beating after each addition, then the vanilla extract. Fold in the flour with a large metal spoon, then stir in the milk and mix well.

3. Divide the sponge mixture between the prepared tins and bake in the oven for 20 minutes, until lightly golden and springy to the touch. Leave to cool in the tins for a few minutes, then turn out on to a wire rack to cool completely.

4. Meanwhile, make the buttercream. Beat together the butter, icing sugar and vanilla extract in a mixing bowl until light and creamy.

5. Spread the jam over the top of one of the sponges. Place the second sponge on top and press down gently. Spread the buttercream on the top of the cake and then decorate with sweets or chocolates of your choice.

Orange polenta cake with golden syrup

This always reminds me of the sponge and golden syrup I used to have for school lunch. We were given a nice wedge of dry sponge, but never enough syrup – which is why I now always make sure there's extra!

Serves 8

250g (9oz) unsalted butter, softened, plus extra for greasing
250g (9oz) caster sugar
3 large free-range eggs, beaten
100g (3½oz) fine polenta
250g (9oz) ground almonds
1 tsp baking powder
finely grated zest of 2 unwaxed oranges and juice of 1
4 tbsp golden syrup

1. Preheat the oven to 180°C/fan 160°C/gas mark 4. Lightly grease a 23cm (9in) springform cake tin and line the base with parchment paper.

2. Beat together the butter and sugar using a food mixer with a paddle attachment, or with a wooden spoon in a large mixing bowl, until pale and fluffy. Add the eggs a little at a time, beating after each addition, then fold in the polenta, ground almonds and baking powder with a large metal spoon. Stir in the orange zest and juice until well incorporated.

3. Tip the cake mixture into the prepared tin and lightly tap on the work surface to level out the mixture. Bake in the oven for 1–1¼ hours, until the cake has risen and is golden. If you find that the top is getting too dark, cover with foil.

4. Remove the cake from the oven and leave to cool in the tin for 5 minutes before removing from the tin and placing on a wire rack. Just before serving, heat the golden syrup in a small saucepan until really loose and warm, then drizzle over the cake, putting a plate underneath the rack to catch the drips.

Orange & poppy seed cake

This cake is something a little bit different, with a citrus-flavoured sponge that's especially light and fresh tasting.

Serves 8

For the sponge
185g (6½oz) unsalted butter, softened, plus extra for greasing
30g (1oz) poppy seeds
4 tbsp milk
½ tbsp finely grated unwaxed orange zest
½ tbsp finely grated unwaxed lemon zest
220g (7¾oz) caster sugar
3 large free-range eggs
225g (8oz) self-raising flour, sifted
75g (2¾oz) plain flour, sifted
60g (2¼oz) ground almonds
100ml (3½fl oz) orange juice
25ml (1fl oz) lemon juice

For the orange syrup
110g (4oz) caster sugar
75ml (2½fl oz) orange juice
40ml (1½fl oz) water
pared zest of ½ unwaxed orange, cut into thin strips

1. Preheat the oven to 200°C/fan 180°C/gas mark 6. Lightly grease a 22cm (8½in) round cake tin and line the base with parchment paper.

2. Start by soaking the poppy seeds for the sponge in the milk for 20 minutes.

3. Beat together the butter, grated orange and lemon zest and sugar using a food mixer with a paddle attachment, or with a wooden spoon in a large mixing bowl, until pale and fluffy. Add the eggs one at a time, beating after each addition. Fold in the flours and ground almonds with a large metal spoon, then stir in the orange and lemon juice and poppy seeds with their soaking milk.

4. Turn the sponge mixture into the prepared cake tin and lightly tap on the work surface to level off the top of the mixture. Bake in the oven for 40–45 minutes, or until golden brown, slightly shrinking away from the edge of the tin, springy to the touch and a skewer inserted into the centre comes out clean.

5. Meanwhile, heat all the syrup ingredients together in a saucepan over a gentle heat until all the sugar has dissolved and the zest has softened.

6. Remove the cake from the oven and leave to cool for 5 minutes before removing from the tin and placing on a wire rack set over a plate. Pour the warm syrup all over the cake. Re-pour any syrup that collects in the plate underneath over the cake. This is delicious served warm.

Banana & pineapple cake with cream cheese frosting

I like to think that the fruit this cake contains and its low-fat cream cheese frosting makes it healthy, so I can justify having a large slice of it – well, it makes me feel less guilty, in any case!

Makes 8 large slices

For the sponge mixture
butter, for greasing
150ml (¼ pint) groundnut oil
250g (9oz) caster sugar
2 bananas, roughly chopped into
    small pieces
130g (4½oz) fresh pineapple flesh,
    roughly chopped
3 large free-range eggs, at room
    temperature, separated and
    yolks beaten
3 tbsp milk
200g (7oz) plain flour, sifted
1 tsp baking powder
¾ tsp ground ginger
¾ tsp ground cinnamon

For the frosting
180g (6¼oz) unsalted butter,
    softened
150g (5½oz) icing sugar, sifted
450g (1lb) low-fat cream cheese
1 tsp vanilla extract

1. Preheat the oven to 200°C/fan 180°C/gas mark 6. Lightly grease a 20cm (8in) round 9cm (3½in) deep springform cake tin and line the base with parchment paper.

2. Mix together the groundnut oil, sugar, banana and pineapple using a food mixer with a paddle attachment, or with a wooden spoon in a large mixing bowl. Add the egg yolks and milk a little at a time, beating after each addition. Fold in the flour, baking powder and spices with a large metal spoon.

3. Put the egg whites in a very clean large mixing bowl and whisk briskly with an electric whisk until they form stiff peaks. Gradually fold the whisked egg whites into the cake mixture, trying not to knock too much air out of them as you do so. Pour the cake mixture into the prepared tin and lightly tap on the work surface to level off the top. Bake in the oven, setting the timer for 30 minutes.

4. Cover the top of the cake tin with foil to prevent the sponge from overbrowning and set the timer for a further 30 minutes. It is quite tricky to test whether this cake is cooked with a skewer, as the banana makes it remain very moist, so you will need to depend heavily on the timings and look to see when the sponge starts to shrink away from the edge of the tin.

5. When the cake is baked, remove from the oven and place on a wire rack. Remove the side collar but leave the cake on the tin base to cool.

6. Using a bread knife, slice the cake horizontally into 3 evenly sized discs. Lay each out on the wire rack to ensure that they cool completely before adding the frosting.

7. To make the frosting, beat together the butter and icing sugar in a mixing bowl with a hand whisk or electric whisk until pale and fluffy. Add the cream cheese and vanilla extract and whisk until you have a smooth paste. Spread an equal quantity of the frosting on to the bottom and middle sponge layers and then sandwich the 3 sponge layers together. Spread the remaining frosting over the top layer of the cake, making sure that you take it right to the edge so that it looks totally indulgent and sumptuous! Make swirls with a fork in the top of the frosting or simply smooth it out.

Cherry & almond buttermilk muffins

My son Jack is such a fan of cherry loaf that he persuaded me to make cherry muffins for the days when he leaves early for swimming training, and he thoroughly approves of the results!

Makes
12 muffins

1 large free-range egg, lightly beaten
180ml (6fl oz) buttermilk
1 tsp almond extract
160ml (5½fl oz) sunflower oil
325g (11½oz) plain flour
150g (5½oz) caster sugar
2 tsp baking powder
½ tsp bicarbonate of soda
¼ tsp salt
250g (9oz) fresh cherries, stoned and halved
25g (1oz) flaked almonds
1 tbsp demerara sugar

1. Preheat the oven to 200°C/fan 180°C/gas mark 6. Line a 12-hole muffin tin with paper muffin cases.

2. Put the egg, buttermilk, almond extract and sunflower oil in a mixing bowl. In a separate bowl, combine the flour, caster sugar, baking powder, bicarbonate of soda and salt.

3. Gently fold the cherries into the dry ingredients. Using a spatula, fold the wet ingredients into the dry ingredients and stir only until the ingredients are just combined – don't overmix.

4. Fill each paper case until almost full with the muffin mixture. Scatter the tops with the flaked almonds and demerara sugar.

5. Bake the muffins in the oven for 20 minutes, until well risen and golden brown. Remove from the oven and leave to cool on a wire rack.

Spiced carrot & raisin cupcakes

A great snack to make a day ahead, these cupcakes stay really moist and delicious. They are perfect for fuelling up your kids before a football game or netball match.

Makes
24 cupcakes

For the sponge
175ml (6fl oz) sunflower oil
175g (6oz) soft dark brown sugar
3 large free-range eggs
150g (5½oz) plain flour
¾ tsp bicarbonate of soda
¾ tsp baking powder
1 tsp ground cinnamon
½ tsp ground nutmeg
220g (7¾oz) peeled and grated carrot
75g (2¾oz) raisins

For the frosting
90g (3¼oz) unsalted butter, softened
75g (2¾oz) icing sugar, sifted
200g (7oz) low-fat cream cheese
1 tsp vanilla extract
2 tsp finely grated orange zest, plus extra
   to decorate

1. Preheat the oven to 200°C/fan 180°C/gas mark 6. Line two 12-hole cupcake tins with paper cupcake cases.

2. For the sponge mixture, put the sunflower oil, sugar and eggs in a large mixing bowl and beat together until well mixed. Sift in the dry ingredients and stir well, then add the grated carrot with the raisins and evenly mix them through.

3. Divide the mixture between the cupcake cases, filling them about half to three-quarters full. Bake in the oven for 18–20 minutes, or until the sponge springs back to the touch of a fingertip.

4. Remove the cupcakes from the oven, transfer them in their paper cases to a wire rack and leave to cool completely.

5. Meanwhile, put all the frosting ingredients in a large mixing bowl and briskly whisk together with a hand whisk or electric whisk until completely smooth. Cover the bowl with clingfilm and place in the refrigerator to firm up for 15–20 minutes.

6. When the cupcakes have cooled completely, gently spoon a generous amount (about 1 tbsp) of the frosting on to the top of each and smooth with a knife. Decorate the tops of the cupcakes with extra pieces of orange zest.

Biscuits & traybakes

Custard creams

This recipe was tricky to get just right – there is a certain pressure when trying to re-create old favourites, but I think I did a good job with this one! The ultimate test is to dip the biscuits into a cup of tea.

Makes approximately 25 biscuits

For the biscuit dough
250g (9oz) unsalted butter, softened, plus extra for greasing
200g (7oz) caster sugar
1 large free-range egg, beaten
1 tsp vanilla extract
350g (12oz) plain flour, sifted, plus extra for dusting
70g (2½oz) custard powder
1½ tsp baking powder

For the buttercream
25g (1oz) unsalted butter, softened
140g (5oz) icing sugar, sifted
2 tbsp condensed milk
½ tsp vanilla extract

1. For the biscuits, beat together the butter and sugar using a food mixer with a paddle attachment, or with a wooden spoon in a large mixing bowl, until pale and fluffy. Beat in the egg and vanilla extract, then fold in the dry ingredients with a large metal spoon – the mixture will come together to form a biscuit dough. Wrap the dough in clingfilm and place in the refrigerator to chill for at least 30 minutes and up to a maximum of 24 hours. Preheat the oven to 200°C/fan 180°C/gas mark 6.

2. You'll need to cook the biscuits in 2 batches. Roll out half the biscuit dough with a rolling pin on a lightly floured surface until about 5mm (¼in) thick. Lightly grease 2 baking sheets and line with parchment paper. Use a biscuit cutter of your choice – I used a heart cutter about 5cm (2in) in diameter – to cut out shapes, and place these on the lined baking sheets.

3. Bake the biscuits in the oven for 10-12 minutes, until lightly golden. Take care not to overcook them, as this will make them brittle – they are best when still slightly chewy in the centre. Remove from the oven and immediately transfer to a wire rack to cool. Grease and line the 2 baking sheets again and repeat the whole process with the second batch of biscuit dough.

4. Meanwhile, make the buttercream. Beat together the butter and icing sugar in a mixing bowl, then beat in the condensed milk and vanilla extract until smooth.

5. When your biscuits are completely cool, spread a fairly generous layer (about 2mm/¹⁄₁₆in) of buttercream on to the domed side of one biscuit (so that the biscuit can sit on its flat underside) and top with a second biscuit, flat side down. Continue sandwiching together the remaining biscuits with the buttercream.

Almond jam cookies

These cookies look so pretty, but they are also easy enough to make with kids – although you should be prepared for everything to end up in a sticky mess in the process.

Makes approximately 30 cookies

185g (6½oz) unsalted butter, softened, plus extra for greasing
1 tsp vanilla extract
165g (5¾oz) caster sugar
2 large free-range egg yolks, beaten
225g (8oz) plain flour, sifted
60g (2¼oz) ground almonds
½ tsp baking powder
2 tbsp apricot jam
2 tbsp raspberry jam
1 tsp grated unwaxed lemon zest

1. Preheat the oven to 180°C/fan 160°C/gas mark 4. Lightly grease 2 baking sheets and line with parchment paper.

2. Beat together the butter, vanilla extract and sugar using a food mixer with a paddle attachment, or with a wooden spoon in a large mixing bowl, until pale and fluffy. Beat in the egg yolks, then fold in the flour, ground almonds and baking powder with a large metal spoon.

3. Take a tablespoonful of the cookie dough, roll it into a ball and place it on a prepared baking sheet. Continue in the same way with the rest of the cookie dough, spacing the balls about 5cm (2in) apart. Using the end of a wooden spoon (or something similar), press a hollow into each ball about 1cm (½in) deep.

4. In 2 separate mixing bowls, mix the apricot jam with ½ tsp of the grated lemon zest and the raspberry jam with the remaining ½ tsp grated lemon zest. Carefully spoon a little of the apricot jam mixture into half the cookies and spoon the raspberry jam mixture into the other cookies.

5. Bake the cookies in the oven for 15 minutes, or until lightly golden. Remove the cookies from the oven and immediately transfer them from the baking sheet to a wire rack, so that their undersides don't overcook. Leave to cool before eating, as the jam gets very hot.

Pistachio & nougat shortbread

This is shortbread with a difference! It's great cut into small, elegant pieces and served with coffee at a dinner party.

Makes
36 small pieces

For the shortbread base
250g (9oz) unsalted butter, softened, plus extra for greasing
120g (4¼oz) icing sugar, sifted
1 vanilla pod, split lengthways and seeds scraped out
1 tbsp caster sugar
300g (10½oz) plain flour, sifted

For the topping
100g (3½oz) shelled pistachio nuts
120ml (4fl oz) condensed milk
120g (4¼oz) dark muscovado sugar
120g (4¼oz) unsalted butter
4 tbsp double cream, plus 2–3 tbsp extra if necessary
200g (7oz) nougat, chopped into 5mm (¼in) chunks
2 tbsp flaked almonds (optional)

1. Start by making the shortbread base. Lightly grease a 20 × 30cm (8 × 12in) baking tin and line with parchment paper. Beat together the butter, icing sugar, vanilla seeds and caster sugar using a food mixer with a paddle attachment, or with a wooden spoon in a large mixing bowl, until pale and fluffy. Fold in the flour with a large metal spoon until a dough forms.

2. Press the dough evenly over the base of the prepared tin and well into the corners until it neatly lines the base. Cover with clingfilm and place in the refrigerator to chill for 30 minutes. Preheat the oven to 180°C/fan 160°C/gas mark 4.

3. Bake the shortbread base in the oven for 20–25 minutes, until lightly golden. Remove from the oven and leave to cool slightly.

4. Meanwhile, make the topping. Put the pistachio nuts in a saucepan along with the condensed milk, muscovado sugar and butter and gently heat until the butter has thoroughly melted, but don't allow the mixture to bubble. Pour the topping mixture over the shortbread base and leave until cool enough to place in the refrigerator. Leave in the refrigerator to set for 30–40 minutes.

5. Heat the 4 tbsp cream in a saucepan over a medium heat, add the chopped nougat and stir gently until dissolved, adding the extra 2–3 tbsp cream if necessary to loosen. Pour the cream mixture over the set sugar and nut mixture. Sprinkle the flaked almonds over the top, if using, and again leave to cool until you can place the shortbread in the refrigerator to set for about 30 minutes. Cut into 36 small pieces and indulge!

Bakewell traybake

This isn't exactly Bakewell tart, but it seems the best way to describe this amazingly delicious treat – great as an after-school pick-up snack before moving on to other activities. I first enjoyed a slice of this in a deli in Sydney, Australia, and had to ask the baker for the recipe as it was so good. I was only allowed to know the ingredients, not the quantities, so I have figured it out by trial and error!

Makes
20 slices

For the shortbread base
175g (6oz) unsalted butter, softened, plus extra for greasing
75g (2¾oz) caster sugar
150g (5½oz) plain flour, sifted
100g (3½oz) ground almonds
finely grated zest of 1 large orange
150g (5½oz) raspberry jam, sieved if you like and well stirred to loosen

For the sponge topping
110g (4oz) unsalted butter, softened
150g (5½oz) caster sugar
4 large free-range eggs, beaten
150g (5½oz) desiccated coconut
75g (2¾oz) ground almonds
1 tsp baking powder
110g (4oz) sultanas

1. Start off by making the shortbread, as this needs to chill. Lightly grease a 22 × 30cm (8½ × 12in) baking tin and line with parchment paper. Beat together the butter and sugar using a food mixer with a paddle attachment, or with a wooden spoon in a large mixing bowl, until pale and fluffy. Fold in the flour and ground almonds along with the orange zest until you have a sticky dough.

2. Press the dough evenly over the base of the prepared tin and well into the corners, smoothing out the surface. Cover with clingfilm and place in the refrigerator to chill for 30–40 minutes. Preheat the oven to 160°C/fan 140°C/gas mark 3.

3. Remove the chilled shortbread base from the fridge and prick the base all over with a fork. Bake in the oven for 20–25 minutes.

4. While the shortbread base is cooking, make the sponge topping. Beat together the butter and sugar, either in a food mixer or by hand as for the shortbread, until pale and fluffy. Add the eggs a little at a time, beating after each addition. Fold in the coconut, ground almonds and baking powder with a large metal spoon, then stir through the sultanas.

5. Remove the shortbread base from the oven and leave to cool slightly. Turn the oven up to 190°C/fan 170°C/gas mark 5.

6. Smooth the raspberry jam over the shortbread base, then carefully tip over the sponge mixture and smooth it over, making sure that you don't push it into the jam layer. Bake in the oven for 20–25 minutes, until the sponge is lightly golden and springs back to the touch of a fingertip. Remove from the oven and leave to cool in the tin, then cut into 20 finger slices.

Blueberry flapjacks

These are great for topping up energy levels on the move. The jumbo porridge oats make them wonderfully substantial and satisfying.

Makes 12 bars

300g (10½oz) unsalted butter, melted, plus extra for greasing
200g (7oz) caster sugar
2 dessertspoons golden syrup
450g (1lb) jumbo porridge oats
200g (7oz) blueberries

1. Preheat the oven to 150°C/fan 130°C/gas mark 2. Lightly grease a 23cm (9in) square 4cm (1½in) deep baking tin and line with parchment paper.

2. Gently heat the sugar, butter and golden syrup in a saucepan, stirring well, until the butter has entirely melted.

3. Place the porridge oats in a large mixing bowl and tip in the melted butter mixture. Add the blueberries and mix together well.

4. Tip the flapjack mixture into the prepared tin and press evenly over the base and well into the corners. Bake in the oven for 35–40 minutes, until golden brown. Remove from the oven and leave to cool in the tin on a wire rack for 15 minutes.

5. Cut the flapjack into 12 oblong bars, transfer to the wire rack and leave to cool completely before either eating all of it or storing in an airtight container!

Oat & cranberry chewy cookies

These cookies provide a great slow-release energy boost, so are perfect for a quick on-the-go snack. They will also store for up to three days in an airtight container.

Makes approximately 40 cookies (enough for a class full!)

225g (8oz) unsalted butter, softened, plus extra for greasing
180g (6¼oz) soft light brown sugar
100g (3½oz) granulated sugar
2 large free-range eggs, beaten
1 tbsp runny honey
2 tsp vanilla extract
175g (6oz) plain flour
1 tsp baking powder
1 tsp ground cinnamon
250g (9oz) porridge oats
140g (5oz) dried cranberries

1. Preheat the oven to 200°C/fan 180°C/gas mark 6. Lightly grease 2 baking sheets and line with parchment paper.

2. Beat together the butter and sugars using a food mixer with a paddle attachment, or with a wooden spoon in a large mixing bowl, until pale and fluffy. Add the eggs a little at a time, beating after each addition, then mix in the honey and vanilla extract.

3. Sift the flour into a separate mixing bowl, add the baking powder, cinnamon and porridge oats and stir together. Gently fold into the wet mixture with a large metal spoon, then stir in the cranberries, making sure that they are evenly distributed.

4. Drop tablespoonfuls of the cookie mixture on to the prepared baking sheets, spacing about 5cm (2in) apart. Bake in the oven for 10–12 minutes, until the edges are turning slightly golden, although they may still be a little soft in the centres, but don't forget that they will continue cooking a bit once removed from the oven. Immediately transfer to a wire rack to cool completely.

Puddings

Swiss roll with raspberry jam

I set out to create a version of a traditional jam roly poly with a suet sponge, but I found it far too heavy. This fatless rolled sponge, by contrast, is light and fluffy, making it a better treat all round.

Serves 8

For the sponge
butter, for greasing
3 large free-range eggs, at room temperature
75g (2¾oz) caster sugar, plus 2 tbsp for sprinkling
75g (2¾oz) plain flour, sifted

For the filling
250g (9oz) mascarpone cheese
5–6 tbsp raspberry jam

1. Preheat the oven to 200°C/fan 180°C/gas mark 6. Lightly grease a 24 × 32cm (9½ × 12¾in) Swiss roll tin and line the base with parchment paper.

2. For the sponge, whisk together the eggs and sugar in a large mixing bowl with an electric whisk, or using a food mixer with a whisk attachment, until thick, pale and creamy, and the whisk leaves a trail when you lift it out of the mixture. Gradually fold in the flour in stages using a large metal spoon, taking great care not to knock the air out of the mixture, until it is all incorporated.

3. Carefully turn the sponge mixture into the prepared tin, then use a palette knife to gently spread it out evenly and smooth off the top. Bake in the oven for 10 minutes, until firm to the touch.

4. Remove the sponge from the oven and set aside for a moment. Cut a sheet of parchment paper slightly larger in size than the Swiss roll tin, lay it on a wire rack and sprinkle it evenly with the remaining 2 tbsp caster sugar. Quickly but carefully turn the sponge out on to the sugar layer, then gently peel away the lining paper. Using the sugar-sprinkled paper and with one of the short ends facing you, roll up the sponge straight away – this will ensure that it is flexible enough to roll without cracking once filled. Leave to cool completely.

5. When you are ready to add the filling, using the parchment paper as leverage, gently unroll the sponge. Put the mascarpone in a small bowl and loosen it by giving it a good stir. Very gently spread the mascarpone over the sponge, then spread the jam on top.

6. With one of the short ends of the sponge facing you, use the parchment paper to help you roll it up and bring up the base, trying to keep the jam and mascarpone from squishing out. Tidy up the finished roll by trimming off the ends.

Apricot & ginger roulade

The filling in this super-light sponge is really creamy but also zingy with the flavours of sweet-spicy ginger and luscious apricot – such a delicious combination.

Serves 6–8

For the sponge
butter, for greasing
4 large free-range egg whites, at room temperature
200g (7oz) caster sugar, plus 1 tbsp for sprinkling

For the filling
500ml (18fl oz) double cream
350g (12oz) organic apricot compote
25g (1oz) stem ginger, finely chopped

1. Preheat the oven to 200°C/fan 180°C/gas mark 6. Lightly grease a 24 × 32cm (9½ × 12¾in) Swiss roll tin and line the base with parchment paper.

2. For the sponge, put the egg whites in a very clean large mixing bowl and start whisking, hopefully with an electric whisk, or using a food mixer with a whisk attachment, otherwise your arms will really ache! As soon as the whites start to thicken, gradually whisk in the sugar. Continue whisking until the whites begin to form peaks and are 'spoonable'.

3. Spoon the egg white mixture into the prepared tin and smooth off the top. Bake in the oven for 15 minutes, then remove and leave to cool slightly.

4. Cut a sheet of parchment paper slightly larger in size than the Swiss roll tin, lay it on a chopping board and sprinkle it evenly with the remaining 1 tbsp sugar. Run a knife around the edge of the sponge and carefully turn it out on to the sugar-sprinkled paper so that the sponge is sandwiched between the sugar-sprinkled paper and the lining paper. Leave to cool completely, then peel away the lining paper.

5. For the filling, whip the cream until it is thick and spreadable, then set aside for the moment. Tip the apricot compote into a bowl and stir to loosen it. Add the stem ginger and stir through. Spoon the compote mixture on to the sponge and spread it evenly, then spread the whipped cream on top.

6. With one of the short ends of the sponge facing you, use the parchment paper to very carefully start rolling, if necessary pushing the cream and compote into the roll, and continue until the sponge is completely rolled up. Trim off the ends to neaten.

Baked cheesecake with rhubarb compote

Baked cheesecake is always a safe bet, and the rhubarb compote served alongside this one complements it perfectly, its slightly sharp taste cutting through the creamy cheese topping.

Serves 8–10

For the base
100g (3½oz) butter, melted, plus extra
    for greasing
250g (9oz) digestive biscuits

For the compote
500g (1lb 2 oz) rhubarb
125g (4½oz) caster sugar

For the cheecake topping
600g (1lb 5oz) cream cheese
2 tbsp plain flour
175g (6oz) caster sugar
½ tsp vanilla extract
2 large free-range eggs
1 large free-range egg yolk
142ml carton crème fraîche, plus 200ml
    (7fl oz) to serve

1. Preheat the oven to 200°C/fan 180°C/gas mark 6. Lightly grease a 20cm (8in) round springform or loose-bottomed cake tin and line the base with parchment paper.

2. Put the digestive biscuits in a food processor and whizz until the mixture resembles fine breadcrumbs, or put them in a double layer of plastic bags and beat with a rolling pin.

3. Transfer the biscuit crumbs to a large mixing bowl, add the melted butter and mix thoroughly. Tip into the prepared cake tin and press down over the base until firm. Bake in the oven for 5 minutes, then remove and leave to cool completely.

4. Meanwhile, for the compote, cut the rhubarb into 2.5cm (1in) pieces. Sprinkle over the sugar and leave to macerate for up to 1 hour.

5. If you have switched the oven off, preheat it again to 200°C/fan 180°C/gas mark 6. Beat all the ingredients for the topping except the crème fraîche together in a large mixing bowl until pale and fluffy. Turn the topping mixture on to the cooled biscuit base and smooth off the top. Bake in the oven for 40 minutes.

6. While the cheesecake is baking, tip the rhubarb into a lightly greased ovenproof dish, cover with foil and bake in the oven for 20–30 minutes, until it is easily pierced with a knife but still holds its shape. Remove from the oven, carefully spoon into a serving bowl and leave to cool to room temperature.

7. Back to the cheesecake, check very carefully that it is set by touching it with a fingertip – it should give slightly but spring back and still wobble, and remember that it will continue to cook a little once removed from the oven. Leave to cool completely in the tin.

8. When ready to serve, very carefully spread a thin layer of the remaining crème fraîche over the top of the cheesecake. Cut into generous slices and serve with a spoonful of rhubarb compote alongside.

Hot apricot & pistachio soufflés

Making soufflés always seems to cause people concern, but these really are very easy to do. The key to success is to be accurate in your timings.

Serves 6

20g (¾oz) unsalted butter, melted
50g (1¾oz) shelled pistachio nuts, finely chopped
25g (1oz) caster sugar
500g (1lb 2oz) apricots, halved and stoned
3 tbsp water
sifted icing sugar, for dusting

For the custard
200ml (7fl oz) milk
1 small vanilla pod, split lengthways
50g (1¾oz) caster sugar
20g (¾oz) unsalted butter
20g (¾oz) plain flour
2 large free-range egg yolks
3 large free-range egg whites, at room temperature

1. Brush the insides of six 7.5cm (3in) ramekins with the melted butter. Mix together the pistachio nuts and caster sugar and use to coat the inside of each ramekin. Place in the refrigerator. Preheat the oven to 200°C/fan 180°C/gas mark 6.

2. Put the apricot halves in a large saucepan with the water and cook for 5 minutes, or until tender. Drain well, transfer to a food processor and whizz until puréed. Pass through a sieve. You will need 200ml (7fl oz) purée.

3. Next make the custard. Put the milk, vanilla pod and half the caster sugar in a saucepan and cook for 2–3 minutes, then remove from the heat.

4. Melt the butter in a separate saucepan over a low heat. When it is bubbling, stir in the flour until it absorbs all the butter. Cook gently, stirring with a wooden spoon, for 1–2 minutes, until you have a smooth paste (or 'roux'). Gradually add the warmed milk with the vanilla pod, stirring or whisking constantly, and cook over a low heat for 2–3 minutes, until thickened and smooth. Remove from the heat and beat in the egg yolks. Turn the custard into a large bowl, cover with clingfilm to prevent a skin forming and leave to cool for 10 minutes.

5. Put the egg whites in a very clean large mixing bowl and whisk with an electric whisk, or use a food mixer with a whisk attachment, until they form soft peaks. Gradually whisk in the remaining caster sugar until the whites are stiff and glossy.

6. Remove the vanilla pod from the custard and then mix in the apricot purée. Gently fold in the whisked egg whites with a large metal spoon. Divide the soufflé mixture between the prepared ramekins, place on a baking sheet and cook in the oven for 12 minutes, until well risen and golden brown. Remove from the oven, dust with icing sugar and serve straight away.

Baked apples

This is something of an old-fashioned dessert. I remember it being a favourite of my granny's, and my mum used to make it too, so it only seemed right to come up with my own version to continue the family tradition.

Serves 4

100g (3½oz) unsalted butter, softened, plus extra for greasing and 4 knobs
   for topping the apples
4 cooking apples
3 tbsp demerara sugar
6 tbsp dried cranberries
4 tbsp desiccated coconut
4 tbsp flaked almonds
finely grated zest and juice of 1 unwaxed lemon
¼ tsp ground cinnamon
double cream, to serve (optional)

1. Preheat the oven to 180°C/fan 160°C/gas mark 4. Lightly grease the base and sides of an ovenproof dish that will hold the apples snugly.

2. Core the apples carefully, making sure that you have removed all the hard area and the pips. Gently score around the middle of each apple to help prevent them bursting as they bake.

3. Place the 100g (3½oz) butter, sugar, cranberries, coconut, flaked almonds, lemon zest and cinnamon in a mixing bowl and mix well to combine. Use to fill the cavity of each apple. Drizzle the lemon juice over the apples and top each with a knob of butter.

4. Bake in the oven for 25–30 minutes, until the apples are soft enough to gently break down and mix with a little cream when served, if you like. Enjoy!

Oven-roasted peaches

This is such a simple dish to make, yet it's so good to eat! The roasting of the peaches intensifies their natural sweetness.

Serves 8

8 tsp unsalted butter, plus extra for greasing
8 ripe peaches, halved and stoned
8 tbsp caster sugar
juice of 1 lemon
8 tbsp flaked almonds, toasted
8 tbsp crème fraîche, to serve

1. Preheat the oven to 220°C/fan 200°C/gas mark 7. Lightly grease the base and sides of an ovenproof dish that will hold the peaches snugly.

2. Place the peach halves, hollow side up, in the dish. Place ½ tsp butter in the hollow of each peach half and sprinkle over the sugar.

3. Bake in the oven for 20–25 minutes, until lovely and tender but not mushy. Squeeze over the lemon juice and scatter over the toasted flaked almonds.

4. Serve 2 peach halves to each person, with 1 tbsp of crème fraîche alongside, drizzled with any remaining cooking juices.

Gooseberry & ginger crumbles

Gooseberries are ideal to use in a crumble because they keep their structure when cooked and so add a satisfying texture to the dish.

Makes 4 individual crumbles

For the crumble filling
800g (1lb 12oz) cooking gooseberries
100g (3½oz) caster sugar

For the crumble topping
75g (2¾oz) plain flour
1 tsp ground ginger
40g (1½oz) caster sugar
40g (1½oz) butter, chilled and cut into cubes
2 tbsp chopped roasted hazelnuts

1. Preheat the oven to 200°C/fan 180°C/gas mark 6.

2. For the crumble filling, top and tail the gooseberries, then give them a wash. Place in a saucepan with the sugar and heat gently for 5–10 minutes, until the sugar has dissolved. Divide the filling mixture between four 250ml (9fl oz) ovenproof pots.

3. For the crumble topping, sift the flour and ginger together into a mixing bowl, then stir in the sugar. Add the butter cubes and, using your fingertips, rub them in until the mixture resembles fine breadcrumbs. Divide between the 4 pots and then sprinkle an equal quantity of the hazelnuts on the top of each.

4. Place the pots on a baking sheet and bake in the oven for 20–25 minutes, until slightly bubbling and golden.

Mini blackberry pavlovas

I love to serve these at a high summer or autumn party, and you can follow the seasons by changing the fruit to match.

Makes approximately 16 mini pavlovas

For the meringues
butter, for greasing
5 large free-range egg whites, at room temperature
250g (9oz) caster sugar
1 tsp cornflour

For the cream
400ml (14fl oz) double cream
30g (1oz) icing sugar, sifted, plus extra for dusting
1 vanilla pod, split lengthways and seeds scraped out
250–300g (9–10½oz) blackberries
sprigs of mint, to decorate

1. Preheat the oven to 180°C/fan 160°C/gas mark 4. Lightly grease a baking sheet and line with parchment paper.

2. Start by making the meringue mixture. Put the egg whites in the bowl of a food mixer with a whisk attachment, or in a very clean large mixing bowl. Turn the mixer, or an electric whisk, on to slow speed and whisk for 1–2 minutes, until the whites begin to froth slightly. Turn the speed up to medium until they start to thicken, then increase to full speed for 2 minutes, until the whites form stiff peaks. Still on full speed, gradually whisk in the caster sugar, a dessertspoonful at a time, until it is all incorporated and the whites are glossy, being careful not to overwhisk. Carefully fold in the cornflour with a large metal spoon.

3. Spoon a dessertspoonful of the meringue mixture on to the prepared baking sheet and pile into a round about 6cm (2½in) in diameter. Carefully make a hollow in the centre of the mound to hold the fruit. Repeat with the remaining meringue mixture, leaving plenty of space between each meringue. Place in the oven and then turn the oven down to 150°C/fan 130°C/gas mark 2 and bake for 20–25 minutes. Turn the oven off and leave the meringues inside for 30 minutes.

4. Remove the meringues from the oven and slide on to a wire rack. Whip the cream with the icing sugar and vanilla seeds until stiff enough to spoon and hold its shape. Place a spoonful in each meringue 'bowl' and top with the blackberries. Decorate with mint sprigs and dust with icing sugar to serve.

Nectarine pavlova

This is a really good-looking dessert, bursting with vibrant colour. The meringue is just the right texture – crisp and light but very slightly chewy. You can make it as neat or 'spontaneous' (messy!) as you fancy.

Serves 4–6

butter, for greasing
5 large free-range egg whites, at room temperature
225g (8oz) caster sugar
300g (10½oz) raspberries
2 tbsp icing sugar
284ml carton double cream
100ml (3½fl oz) crème fraîche
5 ripe nectarines
2 tbsp runny honey

1. Preheat the oven to 150°C/fan 130°C/gas mark 2. Lightly grease a baking sheet and line with parchment paper.

2. Put the egg whites in the bowl of a food mixer with a whisk attachment (it is so much easier to use a food mixer here), or in a very clean large mixing bowl. Turn the mixer, or an electric whisk, on to slow speed and whisk for 1–2 minutes, until the whites begin to froth slightly. Turn the speed up to medium until they start to thicken, then increase to full speed for 2 minutes, until the whites form stiff peaks. Still on full speed, gradually whisk in the caster sugar, a dessertspoonful at a time, until it is all incorporated and the whites are glossy, but be careful not to overwhisk.

3. Spoon the meringue mixture on to the lined baking sheet and pile into a round about 30cm (12in) in diameter, then hollow out the centre slightly, creating a mound around the hollow. Place in the oven and then turn the oven down to 140°C/fan 120°C/gas mark 1 and bake for 1 hour 20 minutes. Remove from the oven and leave to cool completely.

4. Place the raspberries in a blender with the icing sugar and blitz until smooth. Set a sieve over a large bowl and tip the raspberry purée into the sieve. Using a plastic spatula or the back of a spoon, push the raspberry purée through the sieve to remove all the small pips and make a completely smooth coulis. Pour into a jug, cover with clingfilm and refrigerate until needed.

5. Meanwhile, whip the cream until it is really thick. Add the crème fraîche and stir through well. Cut the nectarines in half and remove the stones. Slice each half into 4 wedges and place in a mixing bowl. Spoon the honey over and gently stir to coat the fruit.

6. Spoon the cream mixture into the centre of the cooled meringue and spread evenly, then top with the nectarine wedges, arranging them as fancily or as haphazardly as you like. Drizzle over the raspberry coulis and serve generously.

chocolate

White chocolate & strawberry profiteroles

I love making these, and when they're all piled up ready to serve, it looks like the perfect domestic goddess has been in my kitchen. Add a freshly laundered floral tea towel next to them and we have the perfect scene!

Makes 24 profiteroles

For the choux pastry
100g (3½oz) unsalted butter, plus extra for greasing
300ml (½ pint) water
140g (5oz) plain flour, sifted
pinch of fine salt
4 large free-range eggs, lightly beaten

For the coulis
600g (1lb 5oz) strawberries, washed and hulled
80g (2¾oz) icing sugar, plus extra, sifted, for dusting

For the filling
600ml (1 pint) double cream, whipped
200g (7oz) white chocolate, melted

1. Preheat the oven to 200°C/fan 180°C/gas mark 6. Lightly grease 2 baking sheets and line with parchment paper.

2. Start off by making the choux pastry. Put the water in a saucepan with the butter and gently heat until the butter has melted and the water has reached boiling point. Remove the pan from the heat and immediately tip in the flour, all in one go, with the salt. Beat briskly with a wooden spoon until you have a thick paste that comes away from the side of the pan. Leave to cool for a couple of minutes, then add the eggs a little at a time, beating after each addition, until the mixture is smooth and glossy.

3. Fit a washable nylon piping bag with a 1.5cm (⅝in) plain nozzle, fill with the choux pastry and pipe 12 bun shapes on to each lined baking sheet. Alternatively, simply spoon the pastry into bun shapes. Bake in the oven for 20–25 minutes, or until puffed up and golden. Remove from the oven and leave to cool completely on a wire rack.

4. Now make the coulis. Put the strawberries and icing sugar in a blender and whizz until it is completely smooth. Pour into a jug, cover with clingfilm and refrigerate until you are ready to use.

5. When you are ready to fill the profiteroles, fold together the whipped cream, melted white chocolate and 200ml (7fl oz) of the strawberry coulis in a large mixing bowl.

6. Make a split in the side of each cooled choux bun and either pipe or gently spoon in the filling mixture. Cover the buns with clingfilm and place in the refrigerator to chill before serving.

7. Serve with a little more of the remaining coulis drizzled over the top, if you like, and a dusting of icing sugar.

Soft baked white chocolate, coconut & cranberry cookies

This is a really lovely combination, making a very indulgent cookie. The coconut adds extra interest to the texture – and makes them last a couple of days longer.

Makes about 25–30 cookies

225g (8oz) unsalted butter, softened, plus extra for greasing
200g (7oz) light muscovado sugar
2 large free-range eggs, beaten
1 tsp vanilla extract
300g (10½oz) plain flour, sifted
1 tsp bicarbonate of soda
250g (9oz) white chocolate, chopped into small chunks
100g (3½oz) dried cranberries
75g (2¾oz) desiccated coconut

1. Preheat the oven to 200°C/fan 180°C/gas mark 6. Lightly grease 2 baking sheets and line with parchment paper.

2. Start by beating together the butter and sugar using a food mixer with a paddle attachment, or with a wooden spoon in a large mixing bowl, until pale and fluffy. Add the eggs a little at a time, beating after each addition, then add the vanilla extract. Fold in the flour and bicarbonate of soda with a large metal spoon, then stir in the white chocolate chunks, cranberries and coconut.

3. Place separate tablespoonfuls of the cookie mixture on the prepared baking sheets, leaving 2.5cm (1in) between them, as they will spread a little. Bake in the oven for 10–15 minutes, until golden brown.

4. Remove the cookies from the oven and leave to cool on the baking sheets before transferring to wire racks to cool completely.

Chocolate & hazelnut traybake

This is definitely not a sweet treat for those watching the calories – it's a chocolate feast, and unashamedly naughty and yummy.

Makes 12 brownies

85g (3oz) unsalted butter, melted, plus extra for greasing
100g (3½oz) whole blanched hazelnuts
200g (7oz) plain flour
1 tbsp baking powder
3 tbsp cocoa powder
150g (5½oz) caster sugar
1 large free-range egg, beaten
200ml (7fl oz) buttermilk
4 tbsp hazelnut and chocolate spread, plus 3 tsp for adding to the dents in the brownies
2 tbsp milk

1. Preheat the oven to 200°C/fan 180°C/gas mark 6. Lightly grease a 25cm (10in) square brownie tin that slides apart or is loose-bottomed and line the base with parchment paper.

2. Process the hazelnuts in a food processor, or place in a double layer of sealed plastic bags and beat with a rolling pin, until you have rustic crumbs.

3. Transfer the hazelnut crumbs to a large mixing bowl, sift in the flour, baking powder and cocoa powder together. Add the sugar and stir until well mixed. Add the egg, buttermilk, the 4 tbsp hazelnut and chocolate spread, melted butter and milk, and mix together until you have a lovely bowlful of hazelnut and chocolate goo. Tip this into the prepared tin – it should come halfway up the sides – and using a table knife, mark out into 12 evenly sized squares.

4. Carefully make a small dent in the centre of each brownie, one at a time, and add ¼ tsp hazelnut and chocolate spread.

5. Bake the brownies in the oven for 20–25 minutes, or until spongy to the touch but still gooey in the centre – a skewer inserted into the centres shouldn't come out clean in this case. Remove from the oven and leave to cool in the tin on a wire rack. Once cool, cut into squares.

Chocolate brownie cookies

I love how light and small these cookies are. Since having babies, I have gone off eating rich chocolaty things, so instead of the large cake-style brownies, these deliver just the right amount of chocolate heaven!

Makes approximately 30 cookies

50g (1¾oz) unsalted butter, plus extra for greasing
325g (11½oz) plain dark chocolate (70% cocoa solids), roughly chopped
3 large free-range eggs, at room temperature
175g (6oz) granulated sugar
2 tsp vanilla extract
40g (1½oz) plain flour, sifted
¼ tsp baking powder

1. Preheat the oven to 200°C/fan 180°C/gas mark 6. Lightly grease 2 baking sheets and line with parchment paper.

2. Bring a saucepan of water to the boil and set a heatproof mixing bowl over the pan, making sure that the base doesn't touch the water. Add the chopped chocolate and butter to the bowl, and stir it as it melts until it becomes a smooth, glossy liquid. Remove the bowl from the pan and leave to cool.

3. Whisk together the eggs and sugar in a large mixing bowl with an electric whisk, or using a food mixer with a whisk attachment, until thick and creamy, and the whisk leaves a trail when you lift it out of the mixture. Add the vanilla extract, whisk in the cooled chocolate and butter mixture, then gently fold in the flour and baking powder with a large metal spoon until well incorporated. Leave the mixture to rest for 5 minutes. (You can store the brownie mixture, covered with clingfilm, in the refrigerator for up to 2 hours.)

4. Place separate tablespoonfuls of the chocolate mixture in little piles on the prepared baking sheets – they don't spread very much, but leave about 2.5cm (1in) between them.

5. Bake the cookies in the oven for 8–10 minutes, until the tops have cracked but they still look a little moist – don't overcook, as they will continue to cook a little in the centre as they cool. Remove from the oven and slide on to a wire rack as soon as possible to cool.

Chocolate & beetroot cupcakes

I first tried the chocolate and beetroot combination when I made Diana Henry's cake following her demonstration on the TV food programme 'Market Kitchen'. With the cream cheese frosting crowning the pink sponge, I think these cupcakes look beautiful!

Makes 8 large cupcakes

For the sponge
150g (5½oz) unsalted butter, softened
150g (5½oz) caster sugar
2 large free-range eggs, beaten
100g (3½oz) self-raising flour, sifted
50g (1¾oz) cocoa powder, sifted
125g (4½oz) cooked beetroot, coarsely grated (juices reserved)

For the frosting
280g (10oz) low-fat cream cheese
30g (1oz) icing sugar, sifted
about 1 tsp scarlet food colouring

1. Preheat the oven to 200°C/fan 180°C/gas mark 6. Line 8 holes of a 12-hole muffin tin with large paper cupcake cases.

2. To make the sponge, beat together the butter and sugar using a food mixer with a paddle attachment, or with a wooden spoon in a large mixing bowl, until pale and fluffy. Add the eggs a little at a time, beating after each addition. Fold in the flour and cocoa powder with a large metal spoon, then gently fold in the grated beetroot and its juices until evenly mixed.

3. Divide the cake mixture between the cupcake cases. Bake in the oven for 20–25 minutes, until they spring back to the touch of a fingertip. Remove from the oven and immediately transfer to a wire rack. Leave to cool while you make the frosting.

4. Put all the frosting ingredients in a large mixing bowl and briskly whisk together with a hand whisk or electric whisk until smooth. When the cakes are completely cool, use a palette knife to smooth the frosting over the tops.

Chocolate truffle hearts

These gorgeous truffles would make great little Valentine treats, or simply a romantic after-dinner gesture.

Makes
8 hearts

For the sponge
25g (1oz) cocoa powder
100ml (3½fl oz) boiling water
100g (3½oz) unsalted butter, softened, plus extra for greasing
100g (3½oz) caster sugar
2 large free-range eggs, beaten
75g (2¾oz) plain flour, sifted

For the topping
100ml (3½fl oz) double cream
150g (5½oz) milk chocolate, roughly chopped
chocolate sprinkles, to decorate

1. Put the cocoa powder in a small mixing bowl, pour in the boiling water and whisk with a hand whisk or electric whisk to mix together well. Leave to cool completely.

2. Preheat the oven to 200°C/fan 180°C/gas mark 6. Lightly grease an 8-hole silicone heart mould, each heart about 6cm (2½in) in diameter.

3. Beat together the butter and sugar using a food mixer with a paddle attachment, or with a wooden spoon in a large mixing bowl, until pale and fluffy. Add the eggs a little at a time, beating after each addition. Fold in the flour with a large metal spoon, then stir in the cooled cocoa mixture.

4. Divide the cake mixture between the greased hearts, taking care to fill each only just under halfway, as you want to make very neat little cakes so that they look really pretty.

5. Place the mould on a baking sheet and bake in the oven for 10–12 minutes, until the cakes spring back to the touch of a fingertip.

6. Remove from the oven and leave to cool slightly in the mould on a wire rack. As soon as the mould is cool enough to handle, tip the little cakes on to the rack and leave to cool completely.

7. Meanwhile, make the topping. Heat the cream in a saucepan until gently bubbling. Add the chopped chocolate and then remove from the heat. Stir or whisk briskly until the mixture becomes thick and glossy. Leave to cool and then cover with clingfilm and place in the refrigerator for 30 minutes, until slightly set.

8. When you are ready to finish the hearts, give the chocolate cream a good stir to loosen it slightly. Gently top each heart cake with ½–¾ tsp chocolate cream and smooth into a circle. Decorate with chocolate sprinkles.

Chocolate fudge cake

I have created chocolate cake recipes before, but you can never adapt or try out too many ideas on this theme. This is a great one, with a light sponge and a relatively light filling and icing to match. You may have to make it twice just to test if it's as good as you remembered the first time!

Serves 6–8

For the sponge
175g (6oz) unsalted butter, softened, plus extra for greasing
150g (5½oz) self-raising flour, sifted
30g (1oz) cocoa powder, sifted
1 tsp baking powder
175g (6oz) soft dark brown sugar
3 large free-range eggs, beaten
1 tsp vanilla extract
55g (2oz) plain dark chocolate (70% cocoa solids), roughly chopped

For the fudge icing
200g (7oz) unsalted butter, softened
200g (7oz) icing sugar, sifted
200g (7oz) plain dark chocolate (70% cocoa solids), melted

1. Preheat the oven to 200°C/fan 180°C/gas mark 6. Lightly grease a 20cm (8in) round cake tin and line the base with parchment paper.

2. Place all the ingredients for the sponge in a food processor, or a large mixing bowl, and process, or beat with a wooden spoon, until smooth and slightly pale in colour.

3. Turn the sponge mixture into the prepared tin and lightly tap on the work surface to level it out. Bake in the oven for 55 minutes–1 hour, until the sponge springs back to the touch of a fingertip and a skewer inserted into the centre comes out clean.

4. Remove the cake from the oven, allow to cool in the tin for 5 minutes, then turn out on to a wire rack and leave to cool completely.

5. Meanwhile, make the icing. Put the butter and icing sugar in a large mixing bowl and use a hand whisk or electric whisk to beat together well. Add the melted chocolate and whisk to incorporate it evenly.

6. Cut the cooled sponge in half horizontally. Spread half the icing on top of one cake half, top with the other sponge half and then finish off by spreading the remaining icing thickly over the top of the cake, making decorative swirls in the deliciously naughty chocolate icing. Serve only in large chunks!

Simple melting chocolate pots

This is quite possibly the most amazingly delicious dessert I have ever made! So indulge yourself and your guests – maybe with a little cream to complement.

Serves 4

For the sponge base
150g (5½oz) self-raising flour, sifted
4 tbsp cocoa powder, sifted
50g (1¾oz) ground almonds
200g (7oz) caster sugar
100g (3½oz) plain dark chocolate
   (70% cocoa solids), roughly chopped
   into chunks
175ml (6fl oz) milk
50g (1¾oz) unsalted butter, melted
1 large free-range egg, beaten

For the sauce
2 tbsp cocoa powder
100g (3½oz) dark muscovado sugar
200ml (7fl oz) boiling water

1. Preheat the oven to 200°C/fan 180°C/gas mark 6.

2. Start by making the sponge base. Place all the dry ingredients and the chocolate in a large mixing bowl and stir together. Add the milk, melted butter and egg, and stir together well.

3. Divide the sponge mixture between four 450ml (16fl oz) ramekins or other ovenproof pots or cups – the mixture should fill the pots by just over half.

4. Now make the sauce. Mix together the cocoa and sugar in a mixing bowl, then add the boiling water and stir until the sugar dissolves.

5. Spoon an equal quantity of the sauce on to the sponge mixture in each pot. Place the pots in a deep roasting tin that holds them snugly and fill with hot water until it comes about halfway up the sides of the pots.

6. Bake in the oven for 20 minutes, then turn the oven down to 190°C/fan 170°C/gas mark 5 and bake for a further 5–10 minutes, until the sponge tops spring back to the touch. When you serve and break into the top of the chocolate pots, you will find the gorgeous gooey sauce just beneath the surface.

sweet
pies & tarts

Lemon tart with blackcurrants

Lemon tart has always been my favourite dessert. The addition of blackcurrants not only looks really striking against the lemon curd filling but also softens its bite.

Serves 6–8

For the dessert pastry
(this makes more than you
need but it freezes well)
125g (4½oz) unsalted butter,
   chilled and cut into cubes,
   plus extra for greasing
250g (9oz) plain flour, plus extra
   if necessary and for dusting
50g (1¾oz) icing sugar
2 large free-range eggs
dash of milk

For the lemon curd filling
finely chopped zest and juice
   of 3 unwaxed lemons
60g (2¼oz) unsalted butter,
   softened and cut into cubes
75g (2¾oz) caster sugar
3 large free-range eggs, beaten

For the topping
150g (5½oz) punnet blackcurrants
1 tbsp icing sugar, sifted

1. Lightly grease a 24cm (9½in) loose-bottomed nonstick fluted tart tin and line the base with parchment paper.

2. Start by making the pastry. Sift the flour and icing sugar into a large mixing bowl and add the butter cubes. Using your fingertips, rub the butter in until the mixture resembles fine breadcrumbs. At this stage, either continue with your hands or transfer to a food mixer with a dough hook.

3. Beat together one of the eggs with the milk, add this to the flour mixture and mix until it just comes together into a crumbly ball of dough. Do not overwork it; it should look a little dry. Add a little more flour if needed.

4. Shape the dough into a ball, wrap it in clingfilm and place in the refrigerator to chill for at least 45 minutes or overnight.

5. Roll out the pastry on a lightly floured surface until about 5mm (¼in) thick. Use it to line the tart tin, making sure that you gently press the pastry into the corner and fluted edge. Cover loosely with clingfilm and return to the refrigerator for 30 minutes. Preheat the oven to 200°C/fan 180°C/gas mark 6.

6. While the pastry is chilling, make the lemon curd. Put the lemon zest and juice, butter, sugar and beaten eggs in a saucepan and place over a low heat – it is very important that you don't let the mixture overheat. Heat until the sauce starts to thicken like custard, whisking constantly and without allowing it to bubble, which will take 3–5 minutes. When it is thick enough to coat the back of a spoon, plunge the base of the pan into a sink of iced water to instantly cool it, whisk it for a little longer and then leave in the iced water until needed.

7. Discard the clingfilm from the chilled tart case. Line with parchment paper and fill with baking beans, then 'blind bake' in the oven for 15 minutes, until lightly golden. Remove the tart case from the oven and lift out the paper and beans. Lightly beat the remaining egg and use it to lightly brush the inside of the tart case all over, then return to the oven for a further 5 minutes, to seal the pastry and stop the base from becoming soggy. Remove from the oven and leave to cool completely.

8. Spoon the lemon curd filling into the cooled tart case, spreading it evenly over the base. Arrange the blackcurrants over the filling and dust with the icing sugar to serve.

Bakewell tart with homemade cherry jam

I became hooked on Bakewell slices as a child, so I consider Bakewell tart to be a real treat for my kids. This time I've taken it a step further and devised a fresh cherry jam for the filling, which is delicious and very easy to make.

Serves 8–10

butter, for greasing
250g (9oz) Dessert Pastry
   (see page 75)
plain flour, for dusting
25g (1oz) flaked almonds

For the fresh cherry jam
650g (1lb 7oz) cherries, stoned
50g (1¾oz) caster sugar

For the frangipane
150g (5½oz) unsalted butter,
   softened
150g (5½oz) caster sugar
150g (5½oz) ground almonds
finely grated zest of 1 unwaxed
   lemon
3 large free-range eggs, beaten
   (use some for brushing the
   tart case)
2 tbsp plain flour

For the icing
225g (8oz) icing sugar, sifted
2–3 tbsp water

1. Lightly grease a 25cm (10in) loose-bottomed nonstick fluted tart tin and line the base with parchment paper.

2. Roll out the pastry on a lightly floured surface until about 5mm (¼in) thick. Use it to line the tart tin, making sure that you gently press the pastry into the corner and fluted edge. Prick over the base a few times with a fork, cover loosely with clingfilm and place in the refrigerator to chill for at least 45 minutes.

3. Meanwhile, start making the cherry jam. Reserve 1 cherry for decorating your tart, then put the rest in a saucepan along with the caster sugar. Place over a low heat and cook for about 30 minutes, until the cherries have a gloopy consistency but still retain a little shape. Set aside to cool slightly. Preheat the oven to 220°C/fan 200°C/gas mark 7.

4. Discard the clingfilm from the chilled tart case. Line with parchment paper and fill with baking beans, then 'blind bake' in the oven for 15 minutes. Remove the tart case from the oven and lift out the paper and beans. Lightly brush the inside of the tart case all over with some of the beaten egg that you are using for the filling, then return to the oven for a further 5 minutes, until lightly golden. Remove from the oven and turn the oven down to 200°C/fan 180°C/gas mark 6.

5. Now make the frangipane. Beat together the butter and sugar using a food mixer with a paddle attachment, or with a wooden spoon in a large mixing bowl, until pale and fluffy. Mix in the ground almonds and lemon zest, then add the remaining beaten egg a little at a time, beating after each addition. Sift in the flour and fold in with a large metal spoon.

6. Spread a layer of the cherry jam evenly over the base of the tart case, then top with the frangipane mixture, again spreading evenly. Sprinkle over the flaked almonds in an even layer.

7. Bake the tart in the oven for 20–25 minutes, until golden and firm but still with a spring to the touch. Remove from the oven and leave to cool in the tin.

8. While the tart is cooling, make the icing. Put the icing sugar in a mixing bowl and then gradually beat in enough of the water to make a fairly thick but nice and glossy icing.

9. When the tart is completely cool, spread over an even layer of the icing, making sure that you smooth it off nicely with a palette knife or something similar. Place your reserved cherry in the centre of the tart and set aside until the icing is set before serving.

Almond & blackberry tart

Almonds and blackberries make a great combination of both taste and texture and they look lovely too. This is a good tart to make a day ahead of serving.

Serves 6

butter, for greasing
350g (12oz) Dessert Pastry (see page 75)
plain flour, for dusting
200g (7oz) blackberries
sifted icing sugar, for dusting
vanilla ice cream, to serve (optional)

For the frangipane
175g (6oz) unsalted butter, softened
150g (5½oz) caster sugar
200g (7oz) ground almonds
2 large free-range eggs, beaten (use some for brushing the tart case)
finely chopped zest of 1 unwaxed lemon

1. Lightly grease a 22cm (8½in) loose-bottomed fluted tart tin and line the base with parchment paper.

2. Roll out the pastry on a lightly floured surface until about 8mm (⅜in) thick. Use to line the tart tin, making sure that you gently press the pastry well into the corner and fluted edge. Prick the base lightly all over with a fork, cover loosely with clingfilm and place in the refrigerator to chill for at least 45 minutes. Preheat the oven to 200°C/fan 180°C/gas mark 6.

3. Discard the clingfilm from the chilled tart case. Line with parchment paper and fill with baking beans, then 'blind bake' in the oven for 15 minutes. Remove the tart case from the oven and lift out the paper and beans. Lightly brush the inside of the tart case all over with some of the beaten egg that you are using for the filling, then return to the oven for a further 5 minutes, until lightly golden.

4. Meanwhile, make the frangipane. Beat together the butter and sugar using a food mixer with a paddle attachment, or with a wooden spoon in a large mixing bowl, until pale and fluffy. Mix in the ground almonds, then add the beaten eggs along with the lemon zest a little at a time, beating after each addition.

5. Pour the frangipane mixture into the tart case, level out well, then arrange the blackberries, nicely spaced, in the mixture, pushing them down so that they are sitting in it firmly.

6. Return the tart to the oven and bake for 35–40 minutes, until the frangipane is firm to the touch and springs back slightly. Remove from the oven and leave to cool in the tin on a wire rack for 15 minutes, then carefully remove the tart from the tin. Dust with icing sugar and serve with vanilla ice cream or something equally delicious!

Apricot tart

I first made this on holiday in France when I was helping my mum prepare desserts for a lunch party she was giving. It's another simple sweet tart recipe and ideal to leave for guests to serve themselves. It's also great the next day, served with slightly warmed cream.

Serves 8

butter, for greasing
375g (13oz) Dessert Pastry (see page 75)
plain flour, for dusting
1 large free-range egg
500g (1lb 2oz) mascarpone cheese
2 tbsp icing sugar, sifted
2 large free-range egg yolks
1 tsp cornflour
8 apricots, halved and stoned
2 tbsp apricot jam, well stirred to loosen
1 tbsp caster sugar

1. Lightly grease a 30cm (12in) loose-bottomed fluted tart tin and line the base with parchment paper.

2. Roll out the pastry on a lightly floured surface until about 5mm (¼in) thick. Use it to line the tart tin, making sure that you gently press the pastry into the corner and fluted edge. Cover loosely with clingfilm and place in the refrigerator to chill for at least 45 minutes. Preheat the oven to 200°C/fan 180°C/gas mark 6.

3. Discard the clingfilm from the chilled tart case. Line with parchment paper and fill with baking beans, then 'blind bake' in the oven for 15 minutes, until lightly golden. Remove the tart case from the oven and lift out the paper and beans. Lightly beat the whole egg and use it to brush the inside of the tart case all over, then return to the oven for a further 5 minutes, to seal the pastry and stop the base from becoming soggy. Remove from the oven and leave to cool slightly. Keep the oven on at the same temperature.

4. Put the mascarpone in a large mixing bowl, add the icing sugar, egg yolks and cornflour and stir well. Spread the mascarpone mixture evenly on to the base of the tart case, smoothing off the top. Arrange the halved apricots, cut side up, over the mascarpone filling, pushing them slightly down into the mixture. Brush the apricot jam on to the cut side of each apricot and sprinkle over the caster sugar.

5. Bake in the oven for 25–30 minutes, until the mascarpone mixture is firm. Leave to cool slightly before serving in slices.

Thin apple tart

Slicing the Granny Smith apples really thinly is the only tricky part of making this delicious, pretty tart. Instead of double cream, try serving it warm with a scoop of vanilla ice cream and let it melt into the apple.

Serves 4–6

25g (1oz) unsalted butter, melted, plus extra for greasing
375g (13oz) sheet of ready-rolled puff pastry
plain flour, for dusting
3 Granny Smith apples, peeled, cored and thinly sliced
double cream, to serve

For the purée
2 Bramley apples, peeled, cored and sliced
25g (1oz) unsalted butter
50g (1¾oz) caster sugar, plus 4 tbsp for sprinkling
1 tbsp orange juice

1. Lightly grease a baking sheet and line with parchment paper.

2. Lay the puff pastry sheet out on a lightly floured surface and use a large plate as a guide to cut out a 28cm (11in) round. Transfer the pastry round to the lined baking sheet, cover loosely with clingfilm and place in the refrigerator to chill for 30 minutes.

3. Meanwhile, for the purée, put the Bramley apple slices, butter, 50g (1¾oz) sugar and orange juice in a saucepan and cook over a gentle heat for 10 minutes, or until the apple has softened to a purée. Leave to cool. Preheat the oven to 200°C/fan 180°C/gas mark 6.

4. Spread the cooked apple purée over the chilled pastry, leaving a 1.5cm (⅝in) border of pastry clear around the edge, and arrange the Granny Smith apple slices on top. Brush with half the melted butter and sprinkle over 1 tbsp of the remaining caster sugar.

5. Bake the tart in the oven for 25 minutes. Remove from the oven, brush over the remaining melted butter and sprinkle over the last 3 tbsp caster sugar. Return to the oven for a further 10 minutes.

6. Remove the tart from the oven and leave to cool. Serve in slices with dollops of double cream.

Mulled wine, plum & blackberry pie

Mulled wine is one of my favourite treats – it always conjures up the special atmosphere of Bonfire Night for me. So I've brought its warming, comforting flavours to this fruit pie, where it works perfectly with the plums and blackberries.

Serves 6–8

800g (1lb 12oz) plums, stoned
100g (3½oz) caster sugar, plus 2 tbsp for sprinkling
2 cinnamon sticks
1 vanilla pod, split lengthways
¼ tsp mixed spice
finely grated zest of 1 unwaxed orange and squeeze of juice
75ml (2½fl oz) red wine
2 tsp cornflour, mixed with a little cold water
250g (9oz) blackberries
butter for greasing
500g (1lb 2oz) pack shortcrust pastry
plain flour, for dusting
1 large beaten free-range egg, to glaze

1. Cut the plums into small wedges. Place in a saucepan with the sugar, cinnamon sticks and vanilla pod. Add the mixed spice and orange zest and juice and heat gently for about 4–5 minutes, stirring gently, until the sugar dissolves.

2. Stir in the red wine and cornflour mixture and simmer for a further few minutes until the sauce has thickened and is syrupy. Stir in the blackberries, then warm through until coated with the sauce. Turn off the heat and leave to cool.

3. Lightly grease a 23cm (9in) pie dish. Roll out two-thirds of the shortcrust pasty on a lightly floured surface. Use to line the pie dish, leaving a slight overhang around the edge. Brush the edge of the pastry with a touch of beaten egg and then fill the pie with the cooled plum and blackberry mixture.

4. Roll out the remaining pastry so that it is about 2cm (¾in) larger than the dish. Place the pastry over the filling and pinch around the edge to seal it to the dish, trimming off any excess pastry. Using a sharp knife, make a small hole in the centre of the pie and place in the refrigerator to chill for 30 minutes. Preheat the oven to 200°C/fan 180°C/gas mark 6 and place a baking sheet in the oven to heat.

5. Brush the pie with beaten egg to glaze and sprinkle with the remaining 2 tbsp sugar. Place on the preheated baking sheet and bake in the oven for 25–30 minutes, or until the pastry is golden brown and cooked through.

Open pear & almond crumble pie

I wasn't sure what to call this recipe at first, but it's actually exactly what it says! This is a very hearty dessert, and one that goes down particularly well at Sunday lunchtimes in winter.

Serves 6

3 ripe but slightly firm pears
50g (1¾oz) unsalted butter, plus extra for greasing
juice of 1 lemon
2 whole cloves
1 vanilla pod, split lengthways
3 tbsp soft light brown sugar
½ tsp ground ginger
50g (1¾oz) ground almonds
1 tsp vanilla extract
375g (13oz) pack puff pastry
plain flour, for dusting
15g (½oz) flaked almonds
1 tsp caster sugar
1 large beaten free-range egg, to glaze
double cream, to serve

1. Start by preparing the pears. Peel them and then neatly cut into quarters through the length, carefully cutting out the hard cores.

2. Melt the butter in a saucepan over a medium heat. Add the pears along with the lemon juice, cloves and vanilla pod. When the pears are starting to warm, sprinkle in half the brown sugar and the ginger and let the sugar melt, gently bubble and begin to coat the pears. Cook the pears for a further 6–8 minutes, or until they start to soften but still retain their shape and the sugar is lovely and syrupy. Turn off the heat and leave the pears to cool in the pan. Once cool, remove the cloves and vanilla pod.

3. Preheat the oven to 200°C/fan 180°C/gas mark 6. Lightly grease a baking sheet and line with parchment paper. Mix together the ground almonds, vanilla extract and remaining brown sugar.

4. Roll out the puff pastry on a lightly floured surface until about 1cm (½in) thick and use a plate as a guide to cut out a round about 25cm (10in) in diameter. Lay the pastry round on the prepared baking sheet and lightly prick all over with a fork.

5. Spread the ground almond mixture over the pastry round, leaving a 1.5cm (⅝in) border of pastry clear around the edge. Arrange the pear quarters on the almond mixture as neatly as possible, laying them in a circular formation, reserving one quarter. Slice and use this to fill the centre area. Sprinkle over the flaked almonds and caster sugar, then brush the pastry edge with beaten egg to glaze.

6. Bake in the oven for 20–25 minutes, until lovely and golden – the pastry will rise around the edge and encase the pears. Serve with double cream.

savoury
pies & tarts

Homemade pork & egg pies

These traditional-style pies may involve time, patience and concentration, but you'll find the process satisfying and the result well worth the effort. They're great to make ahead as the centrepiece of a weekend family buffet.

Makes 2 individual pies

2 large hard-boiled free-range eggs
2 thin rashers of smoked bacon
1 large beaten free-range egg,
    to seal and glaze

For the jellied stock
750g (1lb 10oz) pork bones,
    chopped into large pieces
1 pig's trotter, chopped into 4 pieces
1 large carrot, roughly chopped
1 large onion, unpeeled and
    quartered
1 large bouquet garni (sprigs
    of thyme, sage and rosemary
    and a bay leaf, tied together
    with kitchen string)

For the pastry
400g (14oz) plain flour, sifted,
    plus extra for dusting
160g (5¾oz) lard, chilled and cut
    into cubes
1 tsp salt
4 large free-range egg yolks, mixed
    with 90ml (3fl oz) cold water

For the filling
650g (1lb 7 oz) pork shoulder,
    minced
100g (3½oz) pork belly, minced
½ tsp ground mace
½ tsp ground white pepper
1 tbsp chopped sage
pinch of freshly grated nutmeg
salt and black pepper

1. First make the jellied stock. Put all the stock ingredients in a large saucepan and cover with cold water. Bring to the boil and skim off any scum from the surface, then reduce the heat to a simmer and cook, uncovered, for 2 hours. Strain into a clean saucepan and bring to the boil, then again reduce the heat and simmer until you have 300ml (½ pint) left. Leave to cool, then cover and store in the refrigerator until ready to use.

2. Next make the pastry. Put the flour, lard and salt in a food processor and blitz to fine breadcrumbs. Gradually add the egg yolk mixture and mix until a pastry dough forms. (Alternatively, put the flour in a mixing bowl, add the lard cubes and, using your fingertips, rub them in until the mixture resembles fine breadcrumbs, then gradually mix in the egg yolk mixture until it comes together into a dough.) Knead for 5 minutes on a lightly floured surface, then wrap in clingfilm and chill in the refrigerator while you make the filling.

3. Mix all the filling ingredients together in a mixing bowl and season well with salt and pepper.

4. To assemble the pies, divide the pastry dough in half. Roll out two-thirds of each half on a lightly floured surface and use to line 2 loose-bottomed pork pie tins 11cm (4¼in) in diameter. Roll out each remaining piece of pastry into a round to use as a lid.

5. Half-fill each pastry case with filling, taking care to press it down well. Shell the hard-boiled eggs and wrap each in a rasher of bacon and stand upright on the filling. Cover with more meat filling and press down well. Brush the edges of the pastry with beaten egg and place the lid on top, then pinch the edges together to seal. Place the pies in the refrigerator to chill for 2 hours before baking. Preheat the oven to 200°C/fan 180°C/gas mark 6.

6. Make a hole in the top of each pie, brush with beaten egg to glaze and bake in the oven for 50–60 minutes. Insert a skewer into each pie to check that they are cooked through – if the juices run clear and the skewer is hot, the pies are done.

7. Remove the pies from the oven and leave to cool completely in the tins. Carefully remove the cooled pies from their tins. Warm up the jellied stock and use a funnel to pour it into each pie through the hole in the lid. Chill for at least 5 hours in the refrigerator before serving.

Sausage rolls

A spicy twist on traditional sausage rolls, these will last for a good couple of days, so are great to make in batches and then distribute for snacks or lunch boxes.

Makes 12
sausage rolls

375g (13oz) sheet of ready-rolled puff pastry
plain flour, for dusting
1 large beaten free-range egg, to seal and glaze

For the filling
25g (1oz) butter, plus extra for greasing
dash of olive oil
150g (5½oz) peeled shallots, thinly sliced
1 tsp granulated sugar
450g (1lb) pork sausagemeat
2 tbsp finely chopped flat leaf parsley
100g (3½oz) cured chorizo, cut into small cubes
1 tbsp fresh soft white breadcrumbs
black pepper

1. For the filling, start by heating the butter and olive oil in a frying pan, add the shallots and gently fry for about 5 minutes, until softened. Sprinkle in the sugar and continue to cook the shallots over a low heat for about 15 minutes, until caramelized. Remove from the heat and leave to cool. Preheat the oven to 200°C/fan 180°C/gas mark 6. Lightly grease a baking sheet and line with parchment paper.

2. Put the sausagemeat in a large mixing bowl, add the parsley, chorizo and breadcrumbs and season with black pepper. Mix together well.

3. Lay the pastry sheet on a lightly floured surface and cut in half lengthways. Divide the shallots in half and spoon one portion on to each piece of pastry in a 5cm (2in) wide strip lengthways down the centre. Divide the sausagemeat mixture in half and shape each into a sausage shape as long as the length of the pastry, then lay on top of the shallots. Brush the long edges of each pastry piece with beaten egg, then take one long edge and roll around the shallot and sausagemeat to encase, pinch the pastry together to join and cut off any excess. Turn each roll over so that the join is on the underside.

4. Brush beaten egg over the top of the long sausage rolls, then cut each into 6 equal-sized pieces. Place on the prepared baking sheet and bake in the oven for 25–30 minutes, until golden brown. Remove from the oven and leave to cool on a wire rack.

Beef, mushroom & ale pie with Stilton

This makes a great hearty treat. My son Jack considers himself a serious critic of this sort of pie, but he always awards this particular example high marks!

Serves 4

4 tbsp plain flour
salt and black pepper
800g (1lb 12oz) stewing steak, cut into 2.5cm (1in) cubes
5–6 tbsp vegetable oil
1 large onion, sliced
2 garlic cloves, crushed
200g (7oz) button mushrooms, trimmed and halved
1–2 tsp thyme leaves
500ml (18fl oz) fresh beef stock
200ml (7fl oz) dark ale
1–2 tbsp Worcestershire sauce
75g (2¾oz) Stilton, cut into 1cm (½in) cubes
375g (13oz) sheet of ready-rolled puff pastry
1 large beaten free-range egg, to glaze

1. Start by seasoning the flour with salt and pepper, then toss the beef cubes in the seasoned flour.

2. Heat 3–4 tbsp of the vegetable oil in a heavy-based flameproof casserole dish over a medium-high heat. Add the meat, in batches if necessary, and cook until browned all over. Remove from the pan with a slotted spoon to a plate.

3. Add the remaining oil to the casserole and gently fry the onion and garlic for a few minutes to soften. Add the mushrooms and thyme leaves and cook for 5 minutes, until softened but not coloured. Return the beef to the pan with any juices and stir in the beef stock, ale, Worcestershire sauce and a touch of seasoning.

4. Bring to a simmer, stirring, then cover and cook gently for 1½ hours, until the beef is tender. Remove the beef with a slotted spoon to a 26cm (10½in) round ovenproof dish. Cook the sauce, uncovered, over a medium heat for about 10–12 minutes, until reduced and thickened. Pour the sauce over the beef in the dish and leave to cool, then scatter with the Stilton.

5. Preheat the oven to 200°C/fan 180°C/gas mark 6. Once the beef mixture is cool, cut out a round slightly less than 1cm (½in) larger than the ovenproof dish from the pastry sheet and arrange this on top of the pie, pressing or crimping the edge with a fork to seal the dish. Brush the top with beaten egg to glaze and use a sharp knife to prick 3 small holes in the top.

6. Set the dish on a baking sheet and bake in the oven for 25 minutes, or until golden brown. Remove from the oven and serve.

Chicken pie with sweet potato topping

This dish is the ultimate in comfort food. As babies, my children loved both sweet potato and chicken, so this represents the very best of home cooking to them.

Serves 4–6

For the sweet potato topping
500g (1lb 2oz) Maris Piper potatoes, peeled and cut into 2cm (¾in) cubes
900g (2lb) sweet potatoes, peeled and cut into 2cm (¾in) cubes
salt and black pepper
25g (1oz) unsalted butter
2 tsp golden caster sugar
grated zest of 1 orange

For the filling
25g (1oz) unsalted butter
1 onion, diced
1 large leek, trimmed, cleaned and cut into 1.5cm (⅝in) chunks
600g (1lb 5oz) boneless, skinless chicken thighs, cut into 2cm (¾in) chunks
150g (5½oz) chestnut mushrooms, trimmed and sliced
150ml (¼ pint) dry white wine
150ml (¼ pint) double cream
150ml (¼ pint) chicken stock
1 tbsp chopped flat leaf parsley
salt and black pepper

1. Start by making the topping. Cook the potatoes and sweet potatoes in a saucepan of lightly salted boiling water for 10–12 minutes, or until tender. Drain them well and return to the pan. Mash together with the butter, sugar and orange zest. Season with salt and pepper. Preheat the oven to 200°C/fan 180°C/gas mark 6.

2. Meanwhile, for the filling, melt the butter in a large, deep frying pan and gently sauté the onion and leek for about 5 minutes, until softened. Add the chicken chunks and mushrooms and cook for a further 5 minutes, stirring from time to time.

3. Stir in the wine and allow it to bubble and reduce for 5 minutes. Add the cream and chicken stock and simmer for a further 10 minutes, until the mixture begins to thicken. Add the parsley and season to taste with salt and pepper.

4. Spoon the chicken mixture into a 20 × 30cm (8 × 12in) ovenproof dish. Spread the mash over the top of the chicken filling and bake in the oven for 35 minutes, until the mash is well browned and crisp. Remove from the oven, leave to stand for 5 minutes and then serve.

Chicken & corn pies

Using ready-rolled puff pastry, these pies are quick and easy to make, and their creamy chicken filling with the sweet, crunchy addition of sweetcorn should please almost everyone.

Makes
4 individual pies

25g (1oz) unsalted butter, plus extra
  for greasing
2 × 375g (13oz) sheets of ready-rolled
  puff pastry
plain flour, for dusting
1 leek, trimmed, cleaned and finely chopped
1 garlic clove, finely chopped
8 boneless, skinless chicken thighs, cut into
  2cm (¾in) chunks
salt and black pepper
1 tbsp tarragon leaves
150g (5½oz) frozen or fresh sweetcorn
  (frozen are crunchier)
2 tbsp wholegrain mustard
1 large beaten free-range egg, to glaze

For the sauce
50g (1¾oz) unsalted butter
50g (1¾oz) plain flour
300ml (½ pint) milk
300ml (½ pint) chicken stock

1. Lightly grease a baking sheet and line with parchment paper. On a lightly floured surface, make pastry lids for four 325ml (11fl oz) pie dishes by using one of the dishes as a guide and cutting out 4 rounds slightly less than 1cm (½in) larger than the dish from the pastry sheets. Lay the pastry rounds on the lined baking sheet, cover loosely with clingfilm and place in the refrigerator to chill for 30 minutes. Preheat the oven to 200°C/fan 180°C/gas mark 6.

2. Heat the butter in a large frying pan and gently fry the leek and garlic for about 5 minutes, until softened but not coloured. Add the chunks of chicken and cook for 5 minutes, stirring from time to time. Set this pan aside and start making the sauce.

3. Melt the butter in a saucepan over a low heat. When it is bubbling, stir in the flour until it absorbs all the butter. Cook gently, stirring with a wooden spoon, for 1–2 minutes, until you have a smooth paste (or 'roux'). Gradually add the milk and chicken stock, stirring or whisking constantly, and cook until smooth and thick enough to coat the back of a spoon. Stir the sauce into the frying pan with the chicken mixture. Check the seasoning and add salt and pepper as necessary, then stir in the tarragon, sweetcorn and wholegrain mustard.

4. Divide the chicken mixture between the 4 pie dishes and cover with the chilled pastry rounds. Using your thumb and forefinger, pinch around the edge of each pie dish to seal the pastry to the dish, prick the tops of the pies a couple of times with a fork and brush with beaten egg to glaze. Bake in the oven for 30 minutes, until golden and bubbling.

Asparagus, mascarpone & Cashel Blue slices

Cashel Blue cheese is mild and creamy but still has that characteristic bite of blue cheese. It pairs perfectly with asparagus, whose slight crunchiness gives the slice exactly the edge it needs.

Makes 4 slices

1 bunch of asparagus, about 450g (1lb) untrimmed
salt and black pepper
plain flour, for dusting
2 × 375g (13oz) sheets of ready-rolled puff pastry
butter, for greasing
2 large free-range eggs
250g (9oz) mascarpone cheese
200g (7oz) Cashel Blue cheese, cut into 5mm (¼in) chunks

1. Start by trimming and blanching the asparagus. Trim off the woody ends of the spears – approximately the bottom third. Bring a saucepan of salted water to the boil, drop in the trimmed asparagus and simmer for a couple of minutes, until just tender. Drain and plunge into a bowl of iced water – this sets the colour of the asparagus. Set aside for the moment.

2. On a lightly floured surface, cut each of the pastry sheets into 2 evenly sized square shapes, to make 4 in total. Lightly grease 2 baking sheets and line with parchment paper. Place 2 pastry squares on each of the lined baking sheets and carefully score a border about 1.5cm (⅝in) around the edge of each square, then prick the bases with a fork, cover loosely with clingfilm and place in the refrigerator to chill for 30 minutes. Preheat the oven to 200°C/fan 180°C/gas mark 6.

3. Bake the pastry squares in the oven for 10–15 minutes, until golden and the edges have puffed up ready to encase the filling. Remove from the oven but keep the oven on.

4. Mix together the eggs, mascarpone and salt and pepper in a mixing bowl, then divide the mixture between the pastry cases. Arrange an equal quantity of the asparagus on top of each filled tart, and sprinkle over the Cashel Blue chunks. Return the tarts to the oven and bake for 15-20 minutes, until the egg and mascarpone mixture has just set. Remove from the oven and leave to cool slightly before serving.

Crab & chilli samosas

These filo pastry parcels are a little fiddly to make, but they make a light and tasty starter or party food and are especially moreish when served with a sweet chilli dipping sauce.

Makes 16
samosas

2 tsp vegetable oil
1 tsp black mustard seeds
6 curry leaves
1 tsp ground turmeric
1 tsp finely chopped fresh root ginger
1 small red chilli, deseeded and finely chopped
1 small green chilli, deseeded and finely chopped
200g (7oz) canned white crabmeat
1 small bunch of coriander, finely chopped
salt, to taste
270g (9½oz) pack filo pastry sheets, defrosted if frozen
plain flour, for dusting
50g (1¾oz) butter, melted, plus extra for greasing
sesame seeds, for sprinkling
sweet chilli dipping sauce, to serve

1. Heat the vegetable oil in a heavy-based frying pan. Add the mustard seeds, curry leaves and turmeric and fry, stirring, over a low heat for 2–3 minutes, until the mustard seeds begin to pop. Turn off the heat and leave to cool.

2. Place the ginger, chillies and crabmeat in a large mixing bowl and mix together. Add the cooked spices along with the coriander. Season to taste with salt.

3. Preheat the oven to 200°C/fan 180°C/gas mark 6. Lightly grease a baking sheet. Lay 2 sheets of the filo pastry on a clean, dry, lightly floured surface and cut lengthways into 4 strips 7cm (2¾in) wide and 26cm (10½in) long (keep any pastry that you aren't working with covered with a slightly dampened clean tea towel, to prevent it from drying out). Repeat this 4 times to make 16 strips. Brush each strip with melted butter.

4. Place a dessertspoonful of the crab mixture in one corner of each pastry strip and then fold the pastry over into a triangle. Continuing folding the triangle over along the strip until you have a parcel. Repeat this process until you have made 16 parcels.

5. Arrange the parcels on the greased baking sheet, then brush each one with melted butter and sprinkle with sesame seeds. Bake in the oven for 10–15 minutes, until lightly golden. Leave to cool, then serve with a sweet chilli dipping sauce.

Hot smoked salmon and asparagus tart

This easy yet elegant tart features a classic combination of ingredients in its creamy filling. Serve it for an indulgent lunch or a light supper with some lightly dressed salad leaves.

Serves 8

butter, for greasing
500g (1lb 2oz) pack shortcrust pastry
plain flour, for dusting
salt and black pepper
10–12 small asparagus spears, bases trimmed
300ml (½ pint) crème fraîche
2 large free-range eggs and 1 large free-range egg yolk, beaten
3 tsp creamed horseradish sauce
2 tbsp capers, chopped
2 tbsp chopped dill
pinch of cayenne pepper
3 spring onions, chopped
150g (5½oz) hot smoked salmon fillets, flaked

1. Lightly grease a 24cm (9½in) loose-bottomed fluted tart tin and line the base with parchment paper.

2. Roll out the pastry on a lightly floured surface and use to line the greased tart tin, making sure that you gently press the pastry into the corner and fluted edge. Prick the base a few times with a fork, cover loosely with clingfilm and place in the refrigerator to chill for at least 45 minutes. Preheat the oven to 200°C/fan 180°C/gas mark 6.

3. Discard the clingfilm from the chilled tart case. Line with parchment paper and fill with baking beans, then 'blind bake' in the oven for 15–20 minutes. Remove the tart case from the oven and lift out the paper and beans. Return to the oven for a further 5 minutes, until lightly golden.

4. Meanwhile, bring a saucepan of salted water to the boil and blanch the asparagus for 2 minutes, until tender, then drain and refresh in cold water.

5. To make the filling, mix the crème fraîche with the beaten whole eggs and egg yolk in a mixing bowl. Stir in the horseradish sauce, capers, dill, cayenne pepper and spring onions, and season well with salt and pepper.

6. Remove the tart case from the oven. Arrange the flaked hot smoked salmon fillets over the base of the tart. Pour the filling mixture over and arrange the asparagus on top, pushing the spears in gently.

7. Place the tart on a baking sheet and bake in the oven for 25–30 minutes, or until the filling is just set and the top is nice and golden brown.

8. Remove the tart from the oven and leave to stand for 5–10 minutes before removing from the tin and serving.

Tomato galettes

This is one of my favourite savoury tarts – it's sublimely simple and really brings out the best in the flavour of the tomatoes.

Serves 4

butter, for greasing
2 × 375g (13oz) sheets of ready-rolled
  puff pastry
plain flour, for dusting
650g (1lb 7oz) cherry vine tomatoes
4 tsp tomato purée
150g (5½oz) sun-blushed tomatoes
1 red chilli, deseeded and finely chopped
1 garlic clove, finely chopped
1 tbsp olive oil
salt and black pepper

For the dressing
60g (2¼oz) basil leaves, plus extra to garnish
150ml (¼ pint) olive oil
salt and black pepper

1. Preheat the oven to 160°C/fan 140°C/gas mark 3 and lightly grease 2 baking sheets.

2. Lay out the puff pastry sheets on a lightly floured surface and use a small plate as a guide to cut out four 15cm (6in) rounds. Transfer the pastry rounds to the greased baking sheets, cover loosely with clingfilm and place in the refrigerator to chill for 30 minutes.

3. Meanwhile, spread all the cherry vine tomatoes out in a single layer on a baking sheet and roast in the oven for 30 minutes. Remove from the oven and set aside.

4. Turn the oven up to 200°C/fan 180°C/gas mark 6. Lightly prick the pastry rounds all over with a fork and bake in the oven for 10 minutes.

5. While the pastries are baking, blitz the tomato purée and sun-blushed tomatoes to a paste in a food processor, then set aside.

6. Put the roasted tomatoes in a large mixing bowl along with the chilli, garlic, olive oil and a pinch of salt and grinding of pepper. Gently mix together, taking care not to squash the tomatoes.

7. Remove the pastry rounds from the oven. Spread the sun-blushed tomato paste equally over the 4 pastries, then top with the roasted tomato mixture. Return to the oven for 15 minutes.

8. Meanwhile, for the dressing, use the food processor or a stick blender to whizz together the basil leaves and olive oil along with a little seasoning. Pass through a sieve.

9. Serve the galettes warm, with a drizzle of the basil dressing over the top and garnished with salt extra basil leaves.

Summer vegetable & feta tarts

These easy freeform tarts using ready-made shortcrust pastry make a quick and effortless yet impressive lunch.

Serves 4
from 2 tarts

butter, for greasing
2 tbsp olive oil
1 small red onion, sliced
1 garlic clove, finely chopped
1 small aubergine, cut into 1cm (½in) cubes
½ red pepper, cored, deseeded and thinly sliced
½ yellow pepper, cored, deseeded and thinly sliced
1 small courgette, sliced into 5mm (¼in) slices
4 cherry tomatoes, quartered
1 tsp thyme leaves
1 tsp finely chopped rosemary
375g (13oz) ready-made shortcrust pastry
plain flour, for dusting
4 tbsp ready-made basil pesto
70g (2½oz) feta cheese, crumbled
1 large beaten free-range egg, to glaze

1. Preheat the oven to 200°C/fan 180°C/gas mark 6. Lightly grease 2 baking sheets and line with parchment paper.

2. Heat the olive oil in a large frying pan and gently fry the red onion, garlic and aubergine for 3–5 minutes, stirring from time to time. Add the peppers, courgette and tomatoes along with the thyme and rosemary and cook for a further 5 minutes, or until the vegetables have softened.

3. Meanwhile, roll the pastry out on a lightly floured surface until about 8mm (⅜in) thick. Using a plate as a guide, cut out two 20cm (8in) pastry rounds and place one on each prepared baking sheet.

4. Put 2 tbsp pesto in the centre of each pastry round and spread evenly, leaving a 3cm (1¼in) border of pastry clear around the outside.

5. Divide the softened vegetables between the 2 tarts and sprinkle the feta over the top. For each tart, gently lift the border of pastry up and pinch between your thumb and forefinger to partly encase the filling and crimp the edge. Brush around the pastry edge on both tarts with the beaten egg to glaze.

6. Bake the tarts in the oven for 25–30 minutes, until the pastry is golden and cooked through. Leave to cool for 5 minutes before serving.

Mushroom & taleggio tart

Taleggio is a cheese I really love because it's so mild and creamy. I first came across it when I worked at Le Pont de la Tour in their foodstore near Tower Bridge in London when I was studying.

Serves 6

50g (1¾oz) butter, plus extra for greasing
200ml (7fl oz) semi-skimmed milk
142ml carton double cream
1 garlic clove, finely chopped
350g (12oz) new potatoes, peeled and thinly sliced
375g (13oz) sheet of ready-rolled puff pastry
125g (4½oz) mixed crimini and chestnut mushrooms, trimmed and sliced
salt and black pepper
½ tsp freshly grated nutmeg
50g (1¾oz) taleggio cheese (or similar soft cheese), cut into
   5mm (¼in) chunks
crispy green salad, to serve

1. Preheat the oven to 200°C/fan 180°C/gas mark 6. Lightly grease a 23cm (9in) loose-bottomed fluted tart tin and line the base with parchment paper.

2. Put the milk, cream and garlic in a large saucepan and bring to the boil. Add the sliced potatoes and return to the boil, then leave to simmer gently for 15–20 minutes, until the potatoes are tender.

3. Meanwhile, use the puff pastry sheet to line the tart tin, making sure that you gently press the pastry into the corner and fluted edge. Prick over the base with a fork. Line the tart case with parchment paper and fill with baking beans, then 'blind bake' in the oven for 10–15 minutes, until lightly golden. Remove the tart case from the oven, lift out the paper and beans and set aside.

4. While the potatoes are simmering and the tart case is baking, melt the butter in a saucepan. When the butter is hot and bubbling, add the mushrooms and gently fry for 10 minutes, stirring from time to time, until lightly coloured. Add salt and pepper to taste and then set aside.

5. When the potatoes are tender, remove from the heat and season with salt, pepper and nutmeg. Tip the creamy potato mixture into the tart case, sprinkle over the mushrooms and then top with the chunks of taleggio cheese.

6. Bake the tart in the oven for 25–30 minutes, until bubbling and golden. Leave to cool slightly before serving with a crispy green salad.

Meat bakes

stuffed aubergines

It makes a welcome change to use aubergines instead of tomatoes or peppers for stuffing, and they hold the filling really well.

Serves 4

2 large aubergines
1 tbsp olive oil, plus extra for oiling
salt and black pepper
salad leaves and crusty wholemeal
   baguette, to serve

For the filling
1 tbsp olive oil
1 onion, finely chopped
2 garlic cloves, finely chopped
400g (14oz) minced beef or lamb
1 tsp ground cumin
2 tsp curry powder
400g can chopped tomatoes
40g (1½oz) raisins
40g (1½oz) ready-to-eat dried apricots, cut
   into small pieces
small handful of coriander, roughly chopped
salt and black pepper

1. Preheat the oven to 200°C/fan 180°C/gas mark 6.

2. Cut the aubergines in half lengthways and gently score the flesh of each half. Transfer the halves, cut side up, to a lightly oiled baking sheet. Drizzle the olive oil over the flesh and season with salt and pepper. Bake in the oven for 30 minutes.

3. Meanwhile, make the filling. Heat the olive oil in a frying or sauté pan and gently fry the onion and garlic for 5 minutes, until the onion has softened but not coloured. Add the minced beef or lamb and fry over a fairly high heat, making sure that you break it up with a wooden spoon, until browned all over. Add the cumin and curry powder and stir through, then add the tomatoes, raisins and dried apricots. Simmer for 10–15 minutes.

4. Remove the aubergines from the oven and leave until cool enough to handle, then scrape out all the aubergine flesh and roughly chop it. Stir it into the filling mixture, then stir through the chopped coriander and season to taste with salt and pepper. Fill the aubergine cases with the filling – and be generous! Cover tightly with foil.

5. Return the aubergines to the oven and bake for a further 40 minutes, removing the foil for the last 10 minutes of the cooking time. Serve warm accompanied by salad leaves and slices of crusty wholemeal baguette.

Braised short ribs

These slow-cooked ribs make a great alternative to the more familar roasted spare ribs. They are wonderfully tender and so delicious.

Serves 4

4 tbsp vegetable oil
2kg (4lb 8oz) boneless beef short ribs
salt and black pepper
2 carrots, peeled and chopped into 1cm (½in) dice
2 celery sticks, strings removed and chopped into 1cm (½in) dice
2 onions, chopped
1 small head of garlic, cut in half lengthways
4 star anise
2 cinnamon sticks
10 whole cloves
1 tsp coriander seeds
10 black peppercorns, crushed
2 tbsp tomato purée
4 tbsp chipotle paste
2 × 355ml cans Dr Pepper
1 litre (1¾ pints) beef stock, plus extra if necessary

1. Heat the vegetable oil in a large roasting tin over a medium-high heat. Season the short ribs with salt and pepper and sear in the hot oil for 5 minutes on each side, until golden brown. Remove from the tin and set aside. Preheat the oven to 180°C/fan 160°C/gas mark 4.

2. Sauté the carrots, celery, onions and garlic in the roasting tin for about 10 minutes, until caramelized. Add the star anise, cinnamon sticks, cloves, coriander seeds and crushed peppercorns and cook, stirring, for 1–2 minutes, until fragrant. Stir in the tomato purée and chipotle paste and cook for a further 2–3 minutes.

3. Return the short ribs to the roasting tin, pour in a touch of Dr Pepper and bring to the boil while scraping all the browned bits from the base of the tin. Add the remaining Dr Pepper and the beef stock. Cook the sauce for 8–10 minutes, uncovered, to reduce.

4. Cover the roasting tin with foil and roast in the oven for 4–5 hours, until the meat is tender, checking occasionally and adding any extra stock if required.

5. Remove the tin from the oven, lift out the ribs and set aside. If necessary, cook the sauce in the tin on the hob to reduce and thicken. Strain the sauce and adjust the seasoning to taste. Transfer the ribs to serving plates and serve with the sauce.

Fillet steak & spicy burritos

Whenever I make these for dinner, it's a popular choice. Served with the chunky guacamole and creamy crème fraîche – and you can add crispy salad leaves and sliced spring onions too – to complete the indulgence, it's a fantastic meal for a Saturday night in front of the TV, and it's quicker than making lasagne.

Makes 4 burritos

1 tbsp olive oil, plus extra for oiling
1 red onion, finely chopped
1 garlic clove, finely chopped
320g (11¼oz) fillet steak, sliced into thin strips
215g can spicy refried beans
2 tsp chipotle paste
400g can cherry tomatoes, drained
salt and black pepper
4 flour tortillas
120g (4¼oz) mature Cheddar cheese, coarsely grated
½ tsp paprika
4 tbsp crème fraîche, to serve

For the guacamole
2 ripe avocados
juice of 1 lime
½ red onion, very finely chopped
2 tbsp finely chopped coriander
salt and black pepper

1. Preheat the oven to 200°C/fan 180°C/gas mark 6.

2. Heat the olive oil in a large frying pan and gently fry the onion and garlic for 5 minutes, until the onion is softened but not coloured. Add the strips of steak and fry over a medium heat, stirring, for about 2 minutes. Add the refried beans, chipotle paste and cherry tomatoes along with salt and pepper to season. Stir well and leave to cook gently for a couple of minutes.

3. Lay the flour tortillas on a clean, dry surface. Divide the filling between the 4 tortillas, spooning the mixture down the centre of each. Roll up each tortilla into a cigar shape. Arrange on a lightly oiled baking sheet so that the joins are on the underside. Sprinkle the Cheddar followed by the paprika evenly over the top of the burritos.

4. Bake the burritos in the oven for 10–15 minutes, until the cheese is bubbling.

5. Meanwhile, make the guacamole. Slice each avocado in half lengthways, remove the stone and spoon out all the avocado flesh into a large mixing bowl. Mash with the back of a fork. Squeeze in the lime juice, add the red onion and coriander and stir together well. Season to taste with salt and pepper.

6. Remove the burritos from the oven and serve hot, with the guacamole and crème fraîche alongside or placed deliciously and messily on the top – this is never a neat dish!

Baked cannelloni

This was always a dish that I regarded as dry and unappetizing, but by adding a rich, spicy tomato sauce and making sure that it is served in generous portions, it's now the 'X Factor' viewing dinner of choice!

Serves 4
generously

butter, for greasing
16 dried cannelloni tubes
25g (1oz) Parmesan cheese, freshly grated
salad leaves, to serve

For the filling
2 tbsp olive oil
250g (9oz) minced pork
200g (7oz) chicken livers, chopped into small pieces
1 small onion, finely chopped
1 garlic clove, finely chopped
200g (7oz) frozen chopped spinach, defrosted
1 tbsp dried oregano
pinch of freshly grated nutmeg
salt and black pepper
200g (7oz) ricotta cheese

For the tomato sauce
1 tbsp olive oil
1 shallot, finely chopped
1 garlic clove, finely chopped
pinch of salt
good grinding of black pepper
2 × 400g cans chopped tomatoes
1 tsp Tabasco sauce
1 tbsp Worcestershire sauce
handful of basil, roughly chopped

For the white sauce
50g (1¾oz) butter
50g (1¾oz) plain flour
600ml (1 pint) semi-skimmed milk

1. Start by making the filling. Heat the olive oil in a large frying pan over a medium heat. Add the minced pork and chicken livers and cook, breaking up the minced pork with a wooden spoon, for 5–6 minutes, until browned all over. Add the onion and garlic and sauté for 5 minutes, until the onion is softened. Stir in the spinach, oregano and nutmeg and season to taste with salt and pepper. Remove from the heat and stir in the ricotta cheese. Set aside.

2. For the tomato sauce, heat the olive oil in a frying pan over a medium heat. Add the shallot, garlic, salt and pepper and fry for 2–3 minutes, until softened. Add the tomatoes, Tabasco, Worcestershire sauce and leave to gently simmer for 15–20 minutes. Next, add the chopped basil.

3. Meanwhile, make the white sauce. Melt the butter in a saucepan over a low heat. When it is bubbling, stir in the flour. Cook gently, stirring with a wooden spoon, for 1–2 minutes, until you have a smooth paste (or 'roux'). Gradually add the milk, stirring or whisking constantly, and cook until smooth and thick enough to coat the back of the spoon. Set aside.

4. Preheat the oven to 200°C/fan 180°C/gas mark 6 and grease a 25 × 30cm (10 × 12in) ovenproof dish. Using your hands, take a handful of the filling mixture and stuff it into a cannelloni tube. Continue until you have filled all the tubes. Spoon half the tomato sauce over the base of the dish, then lay the stuffed cannelloni tubes on top – they should fit snugly in the dish. Spoon the rest of the tomato sauce over the tubes. Top with the white sauce and then sprinkle over the Parmesan.

5. Bake in the oven for 30–40 minutes, until bubbling and nicely browned on the top. Check that the pasta is just tender and then serve accompanied by salad leaves.

Honey-roast pork fillet

This is a great family dish – just serve it with some stir-fried noodles cooked with freshly cooked tenderstem broccoli to complete the meal.

Serves 4

2 small pork fillets, about 300g
(10½oz) each

For the sticky coating
2 tbsp runny honey
4 tbsp hoisin sauce
4 tbsp dark soy sauce
8 tbsp toasted sesame oil
4 tbsp orange juice

For the noodles
550g (1lb 4oz) dried egg noodles
350g (12oz) tenderstem broccoli
salt (optional)
2 dessertspoons olive oil, plus extra for drizzling
6 spring onions, finely chopped
2 red chillies, deseeded and finely chopped

1. Preheat the oven to 200°C/fan 180°C/gas mark 6.

2. Start by mixing together all the ingredients for the sticky coating in a small mixing bowl.

3. Place the pork fillets in a roasting tin. Pour the sticky coating all over the pork, making sure that it is well covered. You can either roast the pork straight away or leave to marinate in the refrigerator, covered with clingfilm, for 30 minutes. Roast the pork in the oven for 25–30 minutes.

4. Meanwhile, cook the noodles according to the packet instructions. If you have a steamer, steam the broccoli over the top of the noodle pan for 4–5 minutes, until slightly underdone. If you don't have a steamer, cook the broccoli in a saucepan of salted boiling water for 3 minutes.

5. As soon as the broccoli is cooked, tip it into a bowl of iced water to set the colour. Drain the noodles and rinse under cold running water to stop them overcooking, then drizzle over a little olive oil and set aside. Drain the broccoli and cut the stems in half on the diagonal.

6. Check the pork – the sticky coating should be bubbling – and make sure that the fillet is cooked through. Remove from the oven and leave to rest for 5–10 minutes, until cool enough for you to hold and slice.

7. Heat the olive oil in a large frying pan, add the spring onions and chilli and gently fry for 2–3 minutes, until softened. Toss in the broccoli and noodles, and gently stir together until they are all heated through.

8. Carve the pork fillets into thin slices. Spoon the noodles and vegetables on to large dinner plates, top with the pork slices and drizzle with the sticky coating.

Sausage & rosti bake

You can't go wrong with this tasty dish for brunch. It's also great served with a couple of fried eggs on the top.

Serves 6

5 tbsp olive oil, plus extra for oiling
900g (2lb) Maris Piper potatoes, peeled
12 farmhouse sausages
2 red onions, finely sliced
2 tbsp balsamic vinegar
1 tsp granulated sugar
1 red pepper, cored, deseeded and thinly sliced
salt and black pepper
Worcestershire sauce, for drizzling
handful of flat leaf parsley, finely chopped

1. Preheat the oven to 200°C/fan 180°C/gas mark 6. Lightly oil a 26 × 30cm (10½ × 12in) ovenproof dish 6cm (2½in) deep.

2. Place the peeled potatoes in a large saucepan of cold water, bring to the boil and parboil for 3 minutes. Drain and refresh in cold water. Leave to cool and then coarsely grate.

3. Heat 1 tbsp of the olive oil in a large frying pan until shimmering and fry the sausages over a medium heat until browned all over. Remove from the pan and set aside. Heat another 1 tbsp of the olive oil in the pan, add the onions with the balsamic vinegar and sugar and cook over a medium heat for about 5 minutes, until the onions are softened. Add the red pepper and sauté gently for 5 minutes.

4. Meanwhile, place the grated potato in a large mixing bowl, mix with the remaining 3 tbsp olive oil and season with salt and pepper. Spread over the base of the oiled ovenproof dish and bake in the oven for 10 minutes.

5. Remove the potato from the oven. Cover with the onions and red pepper and arrange the sausages on the top. Add a little more seasoning and a good drizzle of Worcestershire sauce, then return to the oven and bake for a further 25–30 minutes, until the sausages are thoroughly cooked through. Sprinkle over the chopped parsley and serve.

Sausage cassoulet

The secret of this recipe is to buy really good-quality sausages – it makes a simple dish really special. It's also a fantastic way to use up any leftover vegetables that may be past their best.

Serves 4 generously

1 tbsp olive oil
8 Toulouse sausages, cut into 2.5cm (1in) chunks
2 small onions, thinly sliced
2 garlic cloves, finely chopped
1 large leek, trimmed, cleaned and finely sliced into rings
1 courgette, roughly chopped
2 carrots, peeled and roughly chopped
2 baby cauliflowers, cut into florets
400g can haricot beans, drained
2 sprigs of thyme
600ml (1 pint) chicken stock
salt and black pepper
125g (4½oz) dried white breadcrumbs, plus extra to serve
handful of flat leaf parsley, finely chopped

1. Preheat the oven to 200°C/fan 180°C/gas mark 6.

2. Heat the olive oil in a flameproof casserole dish with a tight-fitting lid over a medium heat. Add the sausages and cook until coloured all over. Remove from the pan and set side.

3. Add the onions and garlic to the pan along with the other vegetables and cook gently for about 5 minutes, until slightly softened. Return the sausages to the pan, add the haricot beans, thyme and chicken stock and heat until gently bubbling. Check the seasoning and add salt and pepper to taste.

4. Sprinkle the breadcrumbs over the top of the sausages and vegetables, place the lid on the pan and cook in the oven for about 30 minutes. At this point you need to remove the lid and cook for a further 10 minutes, to allow the top to gently brown.

5. Serve the cassoulet on large dinner plates. Sprinkle over the chopped parsley and some more breadcrumbs and serve.

Baked tomatoes

These mozzarella and Parma ham-stuffed baked beef tomatoes make a quick and easy meal. They are also good served after they have been left to cool to room temperature.

Serves 6

6 beef tomatoes
300g (10½oz) mini mozzarella cheese balls
12 slices of Parma ham, torn into strips
6 spring onions, sliced
3 tbsp basil leaves, torn
salt and black pepper
olive oil, for oiling and drizzling
90g (3¾oz) Parmesan cheese, freshly grated
60g (2¼oz) fresh soft white breadcrumbs

1. Preheat the oven to 200°C/fan 180°C/gas mark 6.

2. Slice the tops off the tomatoes, then carefully hollow them out, keeping the outsides intact. Set the hollowed-out tomatoes aside. Chop the tomato flesh and put into a mixing bowl.

3. Add the mozzarella balls, Parma ham, spring onions, basil and salt and pepper to taste to the chopped tomato in the bowl and mix together well.

4. Divide the mozzarella mixture between the 6 hollowed-out tomatoes. Lightly oil an ovenproof dish that will hold the stuffed tomatoes snugly. Arrange the tomatoes in the dish, then mix together the Parmesan and breadcrumbs and sprinkle over the top of the tomatoes. Drizzle with olive oil.

5. Bake the tomatoes in the oven for 20–30 minutes, until they are tender but still holding their shape. Turn the oven up to 220°C/fan 200°C/gas mark 7 and cook for a further 8–10 minutes, until the Parmesan and breadcrumbs are golden. Leave to cool slightly before serving.

spicy chorizo bake

This is another great brunch idea. Its heartiness and spicy chilli kick is especially good for reviving your sense of well-being if you've overdone it the night before.

Serves 4

4 sweet potatoes, peeled and cut into 2cm (¾in) dice
salt and black pepper
2 tbsp olive oil
1 red onion, thinly sliced
2 garlic cloves, crushed
1 tsp paprika
6 fresh spicy chorizo sausages, skinned and crumbled
1 red pepper, cored, deseeded and thinly sliced
2 green chillies, deseeded and sliced into thin rings
400g can chickpeas, drained
10 cherry tomatoes
4 large free-range eggs
Worcestershire sauce, for drizzling
2 tbsp grated mature Cheddar cheese

1. Boil the sweet potatoes in a saucepan of lightly salted boiling water for about 10–12 minutes, or until they are tender. Drain them well. Preheat the oven to 200°C/fan 180°C/gas mark 6.

2. Heat the olive oil in a deep ovenproof frying pan over a medium heat and gently fry the onion and garlic for about 5 minutes, until the onion is softened but not coloured. Stir in the paprika and cook, stirring, for 1 minute. Add the chorizo, red pepper and three-quarters of the chillies, and cook for a further 5 minutes, until the pepper begins to soften. Add the drained sweet potatoes, chickpeas and salt and pepper to taste, and continue to gently fry for another 5 minutes. Use a wooden spoon to mix all the ingredients together well, then press down slightly to line the base of the pan. Add the cherry tomatoes, but just leave them to warm through while remaining whole if possible.

3. Continue to cook until the sweet potato and chorizo begin to turn slightly golden. Sprinkle over the rest of the chillies, then crack the eggs on to the top of the mixture, taking care to keep the yolks whole. Season with salt and pepper and drizzle over a little Worcestershire sauce. Sprinkle over the Cheddar and bake in the oven for about 10 minutes, until the eggs are cooked but the yolks are still runny.

Lamb hotpot

This is the perfect one-pot dish: it requires little preparation and is exceedingly tasty – just the thing to prepare for a school night when hungry kids get home late after swimming and time is short.

Serves 4
hungry children

900g (2lb) best-end lamb cutlets

For the marinade
1 sprig of rosemary
2 garlic cloves, crushed
1 tbsp olive oil
salt and black pepper

For the pot
1 large onion
3 large carrots
1 litre (1¾ pints) lamb stock
3 sprigs of thyme
salt and black pepper
800g (1lb 12oz) Maris Piper potatoes
25g (1oz) butter, melted

1. Preheat the oven to 200°C/fan 180°C/gas mark 6.

2. Put the lamb cutlets in a large bowl along with the all the marinade ingredients, cover with clingfilm and transfer to the refrigerator to marinate while you prepare the vegetables.

3. Slice the onion, peel the carrots and cut them into ½cm (¼in) rounds, and peel the potatoes and cut them into thick slices.

4. Heat a large heavy-based flameproof casserole dish over a medium heat, add the lamb cutlets along with the marinade and cook until browned on both sides. Remove the cutlets from the casserole to a plate and set aside for the moment.

5. Add the onion and carrots to the pan (don't worry if you have any bits of lamb stuck to the base, as this all adds to the flavour) and gently fry for 5–8 minutes, until softened. Return the lamb cutlets with any juices to the pan, add the lamb stock along with the thyme and bring to the boil. Season with salt and pepper.

6. Lay the slices of potato on top of the dish and brush with the melted butter. Bake in the oven for 1½ hours, until the potato slices are nicely browned and tender.

Lamb shanks with white beans

This classic supper dish needs little attention after the initial browning of the meat and sautéing of the vegetables – just leave it to gently bubble away in the oven.

Serves 4

4 meaty lamb shanks
salt and black pepper
3 tbsp olive oil
2 carrots, peeled and finely chopped
1 onion, thinly sliced
2 garlic cloves, finely chopped
1 tbsp chopped rosemary leaves
1 tbsp thyme leaves
300ml (½ pint) red wine
300ml (½ pint) chicken stock
1 tbsp balsamic vinegar
400g can chopped tomatoes
400g can haricot beans, drained

1. Preheat the oven to 200°C/fan 180°C/gas mark 6.

2. Start by seasoning the lamb shanks with salt and pepper. Heat 2 tbsp of the olive oil in a large ovenproof pan with a close-fitting lid over a high heat. Carefully add the lamb shanks – watch out for any spitting fat – and cook for about 10 minutes, until sealed on all sides and with a nice slightly crusty brown surface. Remove them from the pan and set aside on a plate.

3. Add the remaining 1 tbsp olive oil to the pan and gently sauté the carrots and onion with the garlic for about 10 minutes, until the vegetables are softened. Add the herbs, wine, chicken stock and balsamic vinegar, turn up the heat slightly and leave to bubble for about 5 minutes to reduce a little.

4. Tip in the tomatoes and return the lamb shanks to the pan along with any juices. Check the seasoning, place the lid on the pan and cook in the oven for 30 minutes.

5. Remove from the oven, stir the sauce and turn the lamb over, then re-cover and return to the oven for a further hour.

6. Stir in the haricot beans and cook, covered, for a further 20 minutes. Remove from the oven and leave to rest for 10 minutes before serving.

Lamb & lentil casserole

I have to confess to loving the convenience of ready-to-use Puy lentils in vacuum packs. These little pulses are delicious and add the finishing touch to this lamb casserole, which is another great meal you can leave to slow cook.

Serves 6

2 tbsp olive oil
25g (1oz) butter
salt and black pepper
1.2kg (2lb 11oz) boneless shoulder of lamb, cut into 2cm (¾in) dice
1 onion, roughly chopped
1 small swede, peeled and roughly chopped into 2cm (¾in) chunks
3 carrots, peeled and roughly chopped into 2cm (¾in) chunks
2 celery sticks, roughly chopped
1 litre (1¾ pints) lamb stock
3 sprigs of thyme
500g (1lb 2oz) cooked Puy lentils (available ready-cooked in cans
    or in a pouch)

1. Preheat the oven to 200°C/fan 180°C/gas mark 6.

2. Heat 1 tbsp of the olive oil and the butter in a large flameproof casserole with a tight-fitting lid. Add a pinch of salt and the lamb, in batches to avoid overcrowding the pan, and cook over a medium-high heat until browned all over. Using a slotted spoon, remove each batch of lamb from the pan to a plate and set aside.

3. Add the remaining 1 tbsp olive oil to the pan and gently fry the vegetables for 5–10 minutes, until lightly golden and softened.

4. Add the lamb stock to the pan and bring to the boil, then return the lamb along with any juices from the meat and add the thyme.

5. Cover the casserole with the lid, place in the oven and cook for 1 hour, stirring a couple of times during the cooking time.

6. When the hour is up, remove the casserole from the oven and stir in the lentils. Re-cover, return to the oven and cook for a further 30 minutes, until the lentils are cooked and the lamb is tender. Check the seasoning and serve.

Tapenade-coated rack of lamb with Mediterranean cannellini beans

I always think of anything containing beans as comfort food, but this is a surprisingly light dish. What's more, it smells amazingly appetizing while it's cooking.

Serves 2

300g (10½oz) French-trimmed rack of lamb
salt and black pepper
2 tsp olive oil
1 tsp black olive tapenade

For the coating
20g (1¾oz) fresh soft white breadcrumbs
1 tbsp finely chopped flat leaf parsley
1 tbsp freshly grated Parmesan cheese
2 tbsp olive oil

For the beans
1 tbsp olive oil
2 shallots, chopped
1 garlic clove, chopped
1 small red pepper, cored, deseeded and finely chopped
1 small courgette, finely chopped
1 small aubergine, finely chopped
200ml (7fl oz) chicken stock
400g can cannellini beans, drained
25g (1oz) sun-blushed tomatoes
salt and black pepper
1 tbsp finely chopped flat leaf parsley

1. Preheat the oven to 200°C/fan 180°C/gas mark 6. Start by seasoning the rack of lamb with salt and pepper.

2. Heat the olive oil in a large frying pan over a medium-high heat, and when it is slightly shimmering, add the rack, fat side down first, and cook until browned, then turn over and brown the other side. Remove from the lamb from the pan and leave to cool.

3. Spread the tapenade over the fat side of the cooled lamb. Mix all the coating ingredients together well in a mixing bowl and press the mixture on to the tapenade to make the crust. Cover loosely with clingfilm and place in the refrigerator to marinate while you make the beans.

4. Heat the olive oil in a large frying pan and fry the shallots and garlic for 2–3 minutes, until softened but not coloured. Add the red pepper, courgette and aubergine and cook for a further 3 minutes. Stir in the chicken stock, beans and sun-blushed tomatoes, and continue to cook for 10 minutes. Season with salt and pepper and stir in the parsley.

5. Place the rack of lamb, crust side up, in a roasting tin. Cook in the oven for 15 minutes, to give you a medium, pink result; if you prefer it well done, cook for a further 5 minutes. Remove from the oven and leave to rest in a warm place, covered with foil, for at least 15 minutes.

6. When ready to serve, carve the rack of lamb into individual chops and serve on spoonfuls of the bean mixture.

Gremolata chicken Kiev

Chicken Kiev has always been a firm favourite of mine, and this recipe offers a tasty twist on the classic coating. Serve with crisp salad leaves or seasonal vegetables for the perfect dinner.

Serves 6

6 skinless chicken supreme breasts
   (wing bone on)
finely chopped zest of 2 lemons
20g (¾oz) finely chopped flat leaf parsley
125g (4½oz) fresh soft white breadcrumbs
salt and black pepper
4 tbsp plain flour
3 large free-range eggs, beaten
6 tbsp vegetable oil, for frying

For the flavoured butter
200g (7oz) butter, softened
3 garlic cloves, finely chopped
10 sun-blushed tomatoes, finely chopped
salt and black pepper

1. Lay the chicken breasts on a chopping board. Using a sharp knife, carefully cut a pocket in the centre of the long side of each breast.

2. For the flavoured butter, put the softened butter in a mixing bowl, add the garlic, sun-blushed tomatoes and salt and pepper to season and mix together well. Divide the butter mixture between the 6 chicken breasts and firmly pack it into the pocket of each. Cover with clingfilm and leave to chill in the refrigerator until required.

3. Mix together the lemon zest, parsley, breadcrumbs and salt and pepper to taste thoroughly in a mixing bowl.

4. When you are ready to cook the chicken, place the flour, beaten eggs and breadcrumb mixture in 3 separate flat bowls. Take each breast and coat in the flour, followed by the beaten eggs and then the breadcrumb mixture, pushing firmly down on each breast to get as much coating to stick as possible. Lay a piece of parchment paper on a large plate (to stop the coating sticking to the plate), place the coated breasts on the plate, cover and refrigerate for a couple of hours, to help the coating stick and the butter to firm up before cooking. (This is the ideal, but sometimes you may not have time, so just go ahead and cook!) Preheat the oven to 200°C/fan 180°C/gas mark 6.

5. Heat the vegetable oil for frying in a large, deep frying pan over a high heat until hot. Carefully add the chicken breasts to the hot oil and fry each side for 5 minutes, until nicely golden.

6. Remove the chicken breasts to a baking sheet and cook in the oven for 20–25 minutes, until the chicken is completely cooked through – check by using a sharp knife to slice into the thickest part of a breast. Some of the butter will escape as it melts, so simply spoon it over the top of the breasts as you serve. Take care when cutting into the breasts to eat, as the hot butter may spurt out.

Chicken & mushroom pasta bake

Kids always love a pasta bake, especially the way that the pasta becomes crispy and they can just dig in and help themselves. And for something that's so well appreciated, it's also easy to prepare. The ingredients chosen are ever-popular ones, but you can easily change the combination to incorporate leftovers.

Serves 4

salt and black pepper
250g (9oz) dried pasta shells, such
  as lumaconi
2 tbsp olive oil
100g (3½oz) cubed pancetta
1 leek, trimmed, cleaned and sliced
2 garlic cloves, crushed
1 courgette, diced
200g (7oz) chestnut mushrooms, trimmed
  and sliced
100g (3½oz) fresh or frozen peas
2 boneless, skinless chicken breasts, about
  120g (4¼oz) each, cut into 2cm (¾in) dice
3–4 tbsp Madeira
4–6 tbsp freshly grated Parmesan cheese

For the cheese sauce
50g (1¾oz) unsalted butter
50g (1¾oz) plain flour
600ml (1 pint) milk, plus extra if necessary
50g (1¾oz) Gruyère cheese, grated
salt and black pepper

1. Preheat the oven to 200°C/fan 180°C/gas mark 6.

2. Bring a large saucepan of salted water to the boil, add the pasta shells and cook for about 10 minutes, or according to the packet instructions, until *al dente*, then drain.

3. Heat the olive oil in a large frying pan over a medium heat and fry the pancetta until crisp. Remove from the pan with a slotted spoon and set aside. Add the leek, garlic and courgette to the pan and sauté for a few minutes to soften. Stir in the mushrooms, peas and salt and pepper to taste, and cook for 1–2 minutes.

4. Add the chicken to the pan and cook until coloured all over. Stir in the Madeira and cook until evaporated. Add the cooked pasta and mix well.

5. To make the cheese sauce, heat the butter in a saucepan over a low heat. When it is bubbling, stir in the flour until it absorbs all the butter. Cook gently, stirring with a wooden spoon, for 1–2 minutes, until you have a smooth paste (or 'roux'). Gradually add the milk, stirring or whisking constantly, until nice and smooth. Once the sauce is beginning to thicken, remove from the heat and stir in the Gruyère. Season well with salt and pepper, and add extra milk if the sauce is a little too thick.

6. Spoon the pasta mixture into a large ovenproof dish. Pour over the cheese sauce and sprinkle with the Parmesan. Bake in the oven for 15–20 minutes, until browned and bubbling.

Sesame-coated drumsticks

This is a great new take on a kids' special – the sesame seeds make a really crispy coating. My children also like them served with some Tabasco sauce, to add an extra spicy note.

Makes 12 coated drumsticks

200g (7oz) sesame seeds
1 tbsp tahini
1 tbsp toasted sesame oil
1 tbsp olive oil
1 tbsp tomato purée
1 tsp Chinese five-spice powder
1½ tbsp runny honey
½ tsp chilli flakes
salt and black pepper
12 chicken drumsticks

1. Preheat the oven to 220°C/fan 200°C/gas mark 7.

2. Spread the sesame seeds out on a large plate and set aside. Mix together all the other ingredients, except the chicken drumsticks, in a large mixing bowl with salt and pepper to taste. Add the drumsticks, in small batches, and turn to make sure that they are thoroughly coated in the mixture.

3. Gently shake the coated drumsticks and then roll them, one by one, in the sesame seeds. Place the fully coated drumsticks on a rack in a roasting tin and roast in the oven for 30 minutes, or until golden brown and cooked through – check by using a sharp knife to slice into the thickest part of a drumstick.

4. Remove from the oven and leave the chicken to cool on the rack for 10 minutes so that the coating begins to set, then transfer to a plate to cool a little. Serve warm.

Fish &
vegetable bakes

Salmon en croûte with minted pea & bean purée

My daughter Megan has a 'thing' about salmon and is fussy over how she likes it – somehow she always eats it, but not without pulling a face when I say that we're having salmon for dinner. However, this is her favourite way of eating it, so it must be good!

Serves 6

butter, for greasing (optional)
2 × 375g (13oz) sheets of ready-rolled
   puff pastry
2 pieces of skinless centre-cut salmon fillet,
   about 450g (1lb) each, seasoned with salt
   and pepper
plain flour, for dusting
1 large beaten free-range egg, to seal
   and glaze

For the filling
125g (4½oz) frozen peas
125g (4½oz) frozen broad beans
salt and black pepper
20g (¾oz) unsalted butter, softened
small handful of mint leaves
2 tbsp crème fraîche

1. For the filling, start by blanching the peas and broad beans in a saucepan of boiling water with a pinch of salt for 2–3 minutes. Drain and then cool under cold running water. Peel away the skins of the beans.

2. Place the peas and beans in a blender, add the softened butter, mint leaves, crème fraîche and a little salt and pepper (adjust the seasoning to taste after puréeing) and whizz until smooth.

3. Lightly grease a baking sheet and line it with parchment paper. Lay a sheet of puff pastry on the lined baking sheet. Place a piece of salmon in the centre of the pastry sheet, spread the pea and bean purée evenly over the top of the salmon, then place the second piece of salmon on top.

4. Lay the remaining pastry sheet on a lightly dusted chopping board with one short side facing towards you. Using a sharp knife, carefully make a series of 10 horizontal slits in the centre of the pastry where it will lay over the salmon, leaving a border of about 4cm (1½in) around the edge. Brush the pastry border with beaten egg, then carefully lay the pastry, egg side down, over the top of the salmon. Pinch the pastry sheets together, or use a fork to press them together, around the bottom edge to seal the salmon inside the pastry. Carefully brush all over with the beaten egg to glaze. Cover and place in the refrigerator to chill for 30 minutes before baking. Preheat the oven to 220°C/fan 200°C/gas mark 7.

5. Bake in the oven for 25–30 minutes, then turn the oven down to 200°C/fan 180°C/gas mark 6 and cook for a further 10 minutes, until golden brown. Remove from the oven and leave to cool for 10 minutes before serving.

Jersey Royal, salmon & wild garlic tortilla

The Jersey Royals give this flavoursome tortilla a fantastic texture. It's a delicious meal-in-one that is so simple to make.

Serves 4

300g (10½oz) Jersey Royal new potatoes, washed
salt and black pepper
250g (9oz) skinless salmon fillet
500ml (18fl oz) milk
2 tbsp olive oil
1 small onion, finely chopped
6 large free-range eggs
150g (5½oz) fresh or frozen peas
small handful of wild garlic, roughly chopped

1. Put the potatoes in a saucepan, cover with cold water, add a pinch of salt and bring to the boil. Cook for 15–20 minutes, until the potatoes are just tender to the tip of a sharp knife. Drain and leave to cool. Preheat the oven to 200°C/fan 180°C/gas mark 6.

2. Meanwhile, place the salmon in a separate deep saucepan and cover with the milk. Heat until the milk is bubbling, then leave to simmer gently for 2–3 minutes, until cooked through but still soft to the touch. Remove from the heat and leave to cool.

3. Once the potatoes are cool enough to handle, cut them into slices. Drain the salmon, reserving 4 tbsp of the milk, and flake the flesh into a bowl.

4. Heat the olive oil in a nonstick deep ovenproof frying pan, add the onion and potato slices and gently fry for 4–5 minutes, until lightly golden.

5. Meanwhile, break the eggs into a large mixing bowl, add the 4 tbsp reserved poaching milk and whisk together until well mixed. Season with salt and pepper.

6. Arrange the flaked salmon and peas in the pan with the potato and onion, and sprinkle in the wild garlic. Pour over the egg mixture and pop the pan in the oven for 15 minutes, until lightly golden on the top. Remove from the oven and leave to cool for a couple of minutes. Serve either by cutting into wedges in the pan or turning out on to a serving plate.

Oven-baked cod fillets in a puttanesca sauce

This is a sure-fire way of preparing meaty cod fillets without the worry of them overcooking – the sauce keeps them wonderfully moist and helps them to cook evenly throughout.

Serves 2

1 tbsp olive oil, plus extra for oiling and drizzling
2 skinless cod fillets, about 250g (9oz) each
1 banana shallot, finely sliced
1 garlic clove, finely chopped
4 anchovy fillets marinated in olive oil, drained and roughly chopped
1 tbsp capers
350g (12oz) cherry vine tomatoes, sliced
50g (1¾oz) pitted Kalamata olives, roughly chopped
small handful of basil leaves, roughly torn
salt and black pepper
crusty bread, to serve

1. Preheat the oven to 200°C/fan 180°C/gas mark 6.

2. Lightly oil an ovenproof dish large enough to hold the cod fillets and sauce. Lay the cod fillets in the dish.

3. Heat the 1 tbsp olive oil in a frying pan and gently fry the shallot and garlic for 2–3 minutes, until softened but not coloured. Add the anchovies, capers and tomatoes and cook for 10 minutes, until they have just slightly softened. Stir through the olives and basil, and season to taste with salt and pepper.

4. Remove the pan from the heat and tip the contents over the cod fillets. Drizzle over a little olive oil and grind over a touch of black pepper.

5. Cover the dish with foil and bake in the oven for 15 minutes. Remove the foil and bake for a further 5 minutes, or until cooked through – the exact cooking time will depend on the thickness of your cod fillets, so adjust accordingly. Serve with crusty bread.

Halibut en papillote

Cooking fish in parchment paper and foil parcels in this way is an incredibly healthy approach, and locks in all the cooking juices as well as the nutrients.

Serves 2

2 tsp vegetable oil
1 small carrot, peeled and cut into matchsticks
½ small leek, trimmed, cleaned and cut into matchsticks
15g (½oz) fresh root ginger, peeled and cut into matchsticks (reserve the peelings for the stock)
1 small fennel bulb, ½ cut into matchsticks, ½ shredded
1 small red chilli, deseeded and cut into matchsticks
2 skinless halibut fillets, about 200g (7oz) each
2 spring onions, sliced
2 tsp Thai fish sauce
juice of ½ lime
mint leaves, to garnish

For the stock
1 lemon grass stalk, outer layers removed, bruised
2 kaffir lime leaves
2 garlic cloves, sliced
250ml (9fl oz) fish stock

1. Heat the vegetable oil in a small frying pan and gently sauté the carrot, leek, ginger, fennel and chilli matchsticks for 2–3 minutes, until softened. Remove from the heat and set aside.

2. Place all the stock ingredients in a saucepan with the shredded fennel and ginger peelings and simmer for 10 minutes. Turn off the heat and leave to infuse and cool for 20 minutes before straining. Preheat the oven to 200°C/fan 180°C/gas mark 6.

3. Cut 2 squares of parchment paper and 2 squares of foil, each about 28cm (11in). Lay each parchment paper square on a foil square. Place a halibut fillet on each parchment paper square, then divide the sautéed vegetables between the 2 fish fillets. Pour over the strained infused stock. Fold up the edges of the squares to form parcels. Place the parcels on a baking sheet and bake in the oven for 10 minutes.

4. Remove from the oven and open up the parcels. Scatter over the spring onions along with the fish sauce and lime juice, garnish with mint leaves and serve immediately.

Fish lasagne

A fresh, light variation on the traditional meat lasagne, this delicious dish can be prepared in advance on time-strapped days.

Serves 4–6

400g (14oz) skinless undyed smoked
   haddock
1 litre (1¾ pints) milk
100ml (3½fl oz) dry white wine
5 black peppercorns
small handful of parsley stalks
180g (6¼oz) cooked peeled king prawns
180g (6¼oz) cooked shelled mussels
150g (5½oz) frozen sweetcorn
butter, for greasing
9 fresh lasagne sheets
50g (1¾oz) Parmesan cheese, freshly grated

For the sauce
75g (2¾oz) butter
75g (2¾oz) plain flour
1 tbsp chopped dill
salt and black pepper

1. Place the haddock in a large deep saucepan, cover with the milk and wine and add the peppercorns and parsley stalks. Bring to the boil, then turn off the heat and cover with a lid. Leave to infuse for about 10 minutes.

2. Strain the haddock, reserving the milk, and leave the fish until it is cool enough to handle. Flake the fish on to a plate.

3. To make the sauce, melt the butter in a saucepan over a low heat. When it is bubbling, stir in the flour until it absorbs all the butter. Cook gently, stirring with a wooden spoon, for 1–2 minutes, until you have a smooth paste (or 'roux'). Gradually add enough of the reserved poaching milk mixture (about 800–900ml/1⅓–1⅔ pints), stirring or whisking constantly, and cook until thickened and smooth. Stir in the dill and season to taste with salt and pepper.

4. Reserve a third of the sauce, then stir the prawns, mussels and flaked haddock into the remaining sauce along with the sweetcorn. Preheat the oven to 200°C/fan 180°C/gas mark 6.

5. To assemble the lasagne, grease a 22 × 30cm (8½ × 12in) ovenproof dish and line with 3 of the lasagne sheets. Add half the fish mixture, cover with a second layer of 3 lasagne sheets, then top with the remaining fish mixture. Cover with the final 3 lasagne sheets and top with the reserved sauce. Sprinkle over the grated Parmesan.

6. Bake in the oven for 30 minutes, or until golden brown and bubbling. Remove from the oven and serve immediately.

Mackerel fishcakes

These fishcakes are great for making ahead earlier in the day and storing in the refrigerator until ready to bake at suppertime. Serve them alongside some seasonal veg or a crisp salad.

Makes 4
fishcakes

420g (14¾oz) mackerel fillets
300g (10½oz) cooked mashed potato
75g (2¾oz) frozen sweetcorn
3 spring onions, chopped
2 tsp horseradish sauce
salt and black pepper
50g (1¾oz) plain flour
1 large free-range egg, beaten
100g (3½oz) dried white breadcrumbs
25g (1oz) butter, melted, plus extra for greasing

1. Preheat the oven to 220°C/fan 200°C/gas mark 7. Lightly grease a baking sheet.

2. Place the mackerel fillets on the greased baking sheet and bake in the oven for 10 minutes. Remove from the oven and leave until cool enough to handle (keep the oven on), then gently flake the flesh into a mixing bowl, removing any remaining bones.

3. Add the mashed potato, sweetcorn, spring onions and horseradish sauce to the flaked mackerel in the bowl and gently mix together. Season well with salt and pepper. Using your hands, shape the mixture into 4 even-sized fishcakes.

4. Place the flour, beaten egg and breadcrumbs on 3 separate plates. Coat the fishcakes in the flour, followed by the beaten egg and lastly the breadcrumbs, making sure that they have an even coating.

5. Lay the fishcakes on the greased baking sheet and bake in the oven for 10 minutes. Remove from the oven and brush the fishcakes with the melted butter. Return to the oven and bake for a further 10 minutes, until lovely and golden.

Goats' cheese & thyme soufflés

*OK, I am the first to admit that some soufflé recipes can be hit or miss –
I have had my fair share of disasters – but these really are easy to make
and bake, and light too.*

Serves 6

15g (½oz) unsalted butter, plus extra for greasing
2 tbsp fresh soft white breadcrumbs
2 tbsp freshly grated Parmesan cheese
15g (½oz) plain flour
225ml (8fl oz) milk
leaves from 2 sprigs of thyme, chopped
2 large free-range egg yolks
200g (7oz) ripe crumbly goats' cheese, crumbled
salt and black pepper
3 large free-range egg whites, at room temperature

1. Generously grease six 7.5cm (3in) ramekins with butter. Mix together the breadcrumbs and Parmesan and use to coat the inside of each ramekin. Place in the refrigerator while you make the soufflé base. Preheat the oven to 200°C/fan 180°C/gas mark 6.

2. Melt the butter in a saucepan over a low heat. When it is bubbling, stir in the flour until it absorbs all the butter. Cook gently, stirring with a wooden spoon, for 1–2 minutes, until you have a smooth paste (or 'roux'). Gradually add the milk, stirring or whisking constantly, and bring to the boil. Turn down the heat and simmer for 8–10 minutes to cook out the taste of the flour, stirring from time to time to prevent the sauce from burning on the base of the pan. Turn into a large bowl, cover with clingfilm to prevent a skin forming and leave to cool for 10 minutes.

3. Beat the thyme, egg yolks and goats' cheese into the cooled sauce. Season to taste.

4. Put the egg whites in a very clean large mixing bowl and whisk with an electric whisk, or use a food mixer with a whisk attachment, until they form soft peaks. Spoon a quarter of the egg whites into the soufflé sauce to loosen it a little, then fold in the remaining egg whites with a large metal spoon. Divide the soufflé mixture between the prepared ramekins, place on a baking sheet and cook in the oven for 12–15 minutes, until well risen and golden brown. Serve straight from the oven.

Italian gougère bake

I love the classic Mediterranean vegetable and herb flavours of this dish — served with a mixed leaf salad, it makes a perfect summery meal.

Serves 4

For the choux pastry
150ml (¼ pint) water
50g (1¾oz) butter, plus extra for greasing
70g (2½oz) plain flour, sifted
pinch of fine salt
2 large free-range eggs, lightly beaten
75g–100g (2¾–3½oz) Parmesan cheese, freshly grated

For the filling
1 tbsp olive oil
2 banana shallots, finely chopped
1 garlic clove, finely chopped
50g (1¾oz) Kalamata olives, pitted
150g (5½oz) artichoke hearts marinated in olive oil, drained and sliced
270g (9½oz) cherry vine tomatoes
small handful of basil leaves, roughly torn
salt and pepper

1. Start off by making the choux pastry. Put the water in a saucepan with the butter and gently heat until the butter has melted and the water has reached boiling point. Remove the pan from the heat and immediately tip in the flour, all in one go, with the salt. Beat briskly with a wooden spoon until you have a thick paste that comes away from the side of the pan. Leave to cool for a couple of minutes, then add the eggs a little at a time, beating after each addition, until the mixture is smooth and glossy. Stir in 2 tbsp of the Parmesan and leave to cool. Preheat the oven to 200°C/fan 180°C/gas mark 6.

2. For the filling, heat the olive oil in a frying or sauté pan and gently fry the shallots and garlic for 2–3 minutes, until softened. Add the olives, artichoke hearts and cherry tomatoes, and cook for 5–10 minutes, until softened. Stir in the basil and season with salt and pepper.

3. Grease an oval gratin dish 28cm (11in) long and 21cm (8¼in) at its widest point. Spoon the choux pastry mixture all around the outside of the dish and arrange the filling in the centre of the dish. Scatter with the remaining grated Parmesan.

4. Bake in the oven for 25 minutes, until the pastry is golden brown and the filling is bubbling. Leave to rest for 5–10 minutes before serving.

Baked eggs

This very simple supper is delicious served with fresh warm bread –
I love it with the Cheesy Bread Rolls (see page 166):

Serves 4

butter, for greasing
125ml (4fl oz) single cream
1 tsp wholegrain mustard
2 tsp chopped tarragon
salt and black pepper
4 large free-range eggs
fresh warm bread, to serve

1. Preheat the oven to 200°C/fan 180°C/gas mark 6. Lightly grease four 7.5cm (3in) ramekins.

2. Mix together the cream, mustard and tarragon, adding a little salt and pepper to season.

3. Divide the cream mixture between the greased ramekins, then crack an egg into each dish, taking great care not to break the yolks.

4. Place the ramekins on a baking sheet and bake in the oven for 10–12 minutes, or until the whites of the eggs are cooked but the yolks are lovely and runny.

5. To enjoy, either dip the bread into the ramekin or simply tip the contents of the ramekin out on to some thick-cut bread generously spread with butter.

Tomato & chilli jam

This spicy condiment is perfect to serve alongside the Whole Baked Camembert on page 186.

Serves 4

olive oil, for oiling
500g (1lb 2oz) very ripe cherry tomatoes
3 red chillies, roughly chopped (with seeds)
1 red onion, finely chopped
4 garlic cloves, finely chopped
1cm (½in) piece of fresh root ginger, peeled and finely chopped
3 tbsp balsamic vinegar
1 tbsp soft dark brown sugar
salt and black pepper

1. Preheat the oven to 200°C/fan 180°C/gas mark 6. Lightly oil a small roasting tin.

2. Place all the ingredients in the roasting tin, season well with salt and pepper and toss together until well mixed. Roast in the oven for 50 minutes–1 hour, until softened and slightly thickened, but take care not to let the onion burn, as this will leave a bitter taste. Remove from the oven and leave to cool completely.

3. Spoon into a clean jar with a screw-top lid and store in the refrigerator for up to 2 days.

Sweet potato & chilli wedges

Incredibly simple and hugely tasty, these wedges are great with anything from chicken or fish to roasted vegetables.

Makes
24 wedges

2 medium-large sweet potatoes, cut into wedges
1 tbsp olive oil
1 tsp salt flakes
1 tsp chilli flakes

1. Preheat the oven to 200°C/fan 180°C/gas mark 6.

2. Mix together all the ingredients in a large mixing bowl, ensuring that the potato wedges are thoroughly coated in the oil.

3. Spread the coated potato wedges out on a baking sheet and bake in the oven for 40 minutes, or until tender with a crispy outside. These are best served hot.

Deliciously moreish twice-baked potatoes

These filled baked potatoes make a great addition to all kinds of meals, from a summer barbecue to a casual TV supper.

Serves 4

4 large baking potatoes
4 tbsp salt flakes
20g (¾oz) butter, plus extra for greasing
2 tbsp crème fraîche
10 sun-dried tomatoes, chopped
6 spring onions, finely chopped
70g (2½oz) frozen or fresh sweetcorn, defrosted if frozen
   (I use frozen, as it is far crunchier)
100g (3½oz) Cheddar cheese, coarsely grated

1. Preheat the oven to 220°C/fan 200°C/gas mark 7. Cut 4 squares of foil, each large enough to wrap around a potato. Wash the potatoes and pat dry, then prick all over with a sharp knife.

2. Rub 1 tbsp salt flakes into the skin of each potato over a square of foil so that the salt is caught, then wrap the foil around the potatoes and place them on a baking sheet. Bake in the oven for 1½ hours, depending on their size – they are ready when they are soft to the touch. Keep the oven on at the same temperature.

3. Lightly grease an ovenproof dish that will hold the 8 potato halves snugly. When the potatoes are cool enough to handle, unwrap them and discard the foil. Cut the potatoes in half lengthways and carefully scoop out the flesh into a mixing bowl, keeping the skins intact for filling.

4. Add the butter and crème fraîche to the potato flesh and mash together thoroughly. Add the sun-dried tomatoes, spring onions and sweetcorn, and mix well. Spoon an equal quantity of the filling mixture into each potato skin.

5. Place the filled potato skins in the greased dish. Sprinkle over the Cheddar and bake in the oven for 15–20 minutes, until the cheese is bubbling. Eat warm.

Oven-roasted plum tomato soup

Roasting the tomatoes intensifies their flavour and makes all the difference to the taste of this classic soup. This recipe is a prime example of the simpler the better!

Serves 4–6

3 tbsp olive oil
1.5kg (3lb 5oz) plum tomatoes, cut into quarters lengthways
salt and black pepper
small knob of butter
2 onions, finely chopped
6 garlic cloves, finely chopped
1 red chilli, deseeded and finely chopped
400g can cherry tomatoes
large handful of basil, finely chopped
1 tsp thyme leaves
700ml (1¼ pints) chicken stock (adjust the amount as necessary; some tomatoes are much more watery than others)
1 tsp balsamic vinegar
1 tsp Worcestershire sauce
slices of toasted ciabatta, to serve
fresh thyme leaves, to garnish

1. Preheat the oven to 220°C/fan 200°C/gas mark 7.

2. Drizzle 2 tbsp of the olive oil over a large, deep roasting tin, spread over the tomato quarters and season well with salt and pepper. Gently toss the tomatoes to ensure that they are evenly coated with the seasoning and oil. Roast in the oven for 35–40 minutes, until very soft and slightly charred.

3. Meanwhile, heat the remaining 1 tbsp olive oil with the butter in a large frying pan and gently fry the onions, garlic and chilli for 20 minutes, until the onions are soft and golden. Add the cherry tomatoes with their juice, the basil and thyme, and stir well.

4. When the roasted tomatoes are ready, add them to the pan along with any juices and mix together well. Transfer the mixture to a food processor and whizz until smooth, then return to the pan. Add enough chicken stock to give the right consistency, then stir in the balsamic vinegar and Worcestershire sauce. Adjust the seasoning to taste.

5. Heat the soup through and leave to simmer gently for 20 minutes. Serve either hot or chilled, accompanied by slices of toasted ciabatta.

Mini potato pizzas

These are fiddly to prepare, but they make a nice change from bread pizzas and have proved very popular as canapés or party food for my kids – sometimes when we have a Saturday TV night I serve these as a pre-dinner treat.

Makes 24
mini pizzas

600g (1lb 5oz) Maris Piper potatoes, peeled
100g (3½oz) unsalted butter, melted, plus extra for greasing
salt and black pepper
50g (1¾oz) ready-made basil pesto
50g (1¾oz) ready-made tomato pesto
50g (1¾oz) button mushrooms, trimmed and sliced
80g (2¾oz) Parmesan cheese, finely grated
50g (1¾oz) mozzarella cheese, coarsely grated
small handful of basil leaves

1. Place the potatoes in a saucepan of cold water, bring to the boil and parboil for 3 minutes. Drain and refresh in cold water. Leave to cool and then coarsely grate.

2. Preheat the oven to 200°C/fan 180°C/gas mark 6. Lightly grease 2 baking sheets and line with parchment paper. Put the grated potato in a large mixing bowl and stir in the melted butter. Season with salt and pepper. Firmly press 1 tbsp of the potato mixture into a 6.5cm (2½in) round cutter on one of the prepared baking sheets to make a circular disc. Continue until you have used all the potato mixture – you should have about 24 discs.

3. Bake the potato discs in the oven for 20 minutes, turn the discs over and bake for a further 5–10 minutes, until they are all lightly browned.

4. Remove from the oven and spread half the potato discs with the basil pesto and the other half with the tomato pesto. Top with the mushrooms. Mix together the cheeses and sprinkle on top.

5. Return the potato pizzas to the oven and bake for a further 5–10 minutes, until the cheese is melted and bubbling slightly. Sprinkle over the basil leaves just before serving.

Roasted creamed sweetcorn

We all love sweetcorn, however it's prepared, but cooking the corn in this way allows it to steam in the husk in its own moisture. This method also makes it really easy to remove the kernels.

Serves 4

4 corn on the cob, in their husks
25g (1oz) unsalted butter
1 onion, finely chopped
1 tsp caster sugar
$\frac{1}{8}$ tsp freshly grated nutmeg
125ml (4fl oz) double cream
salt and black pepper

1. Preheat the oven to 200°C/fan 180°C/gas mark 6.

2. Place the corn cobs, still in their husks, directly on the oven shelf and roast for 30 minutes, until tender to the tip of a sharp knife. Remove from the oven and leave until the husks are cool enough for you to handle.

3. Meanwhile, melt the butter in a frying pan and gently fry the onion for 5 minutes, until softened. Add the sugar and nutmeg, stir together and cook for a further 5 minutes.

4. Peel back the husk of each corn cob in turn and use it as a handle to hold the cob while you slice off the kernels.

5. Add the corn kernels to the pan, then stir in the cream and season to taste with salt and pepper. Cook gently, stirring, until heated through. Serve hot.

Bread

Sun-blushed tomato & pancetta bread

This is a great breakfast loaf – especially delicious when served as a sandwich with a fried egg in the centre or toasted and cut into soldiers to go with boiled eggs.

**Makes
2 loaves**

150ml (¼ pint) lukewarm water, plus extra if necessary
50ml (2fl oz) olive oil, plus 1 tsp for frying the onion and extra for oiling
25g (1oz) fresh yeast
15g (½oz) caster sugar
140g (5oz) cubed pancetta
1 red onion, finely chopped
20 sun-blushed tomatoes
900g (2lb) strong white bread flour, plus extra if necessary and for dusting
15g (½oz) salt
2 tbsp sun-dried tomato paste, mixed with 200ml (7fl oz) water
small handful of oregano, chopped

1. Mix together the water, the 50ml (2fl oz) olive oil, the fresh yeast and sugar in a small mixing bowl. Set aside for 10 minutes, to allow the yeast to activate.

2. Meanwhile, heat a frying pan over a medium heat and fry the pancetta cubes until golden. Remove from the pan to a plate lined with kitchen paper so that any excess oil is soaked up.

3. Add the remaining 1 tsp olive oil to the pan and fry the onion for about 5 minutes, until softened but not coloured. As with the pancetta, remove from the pan and lay on some kitchen paper to soak up any excess oil.

4. Chop up the sun-blushed tomatoes and also lay on kitchen paper to soak up any excess oil.

5. Place the flour and salt in the bowl of a food mixer with a dough hook. With the mixer on a low speed, pour in the yeast mixture and add the sun-dried tomato paste, pancetta, sun-blushed tomatoes, onion and oregano. Mix until a soft, pliable dough forms, if necessary adding a touch more water or flour accordingly. Continue to knead for about 5 minutes, until smooth and elastic. (If making by hand, place the flour and salt in a large mixing bowl. Make a well in the centre and add the yeast mixture along with the sun-dried tomato paste, pancetta, sun-blushed tomatoes, onion and oregano. Mix until a soft, pliable dough forms, adding a little extra water or flour as necessary. Knead the dough on a lightly floured surface for 10 minutes, until smooth and elastic.)

6. Transfer the dough to a lightly oiled bowl, cover with a clean damp tea towel and leave in a warm place to rise for 40–45 minutes, or until doubled in size.

7. Punch the dough back down in size and divide in half. Form each piece of dough into a round and place on an oiled baking sheet. Cover again with the tea towel and put in a warm place for a further 40–45 minutes, or until doubled in size. Preheat the oven to 220°C/fan 200°C/gas mark 7.

8. Bake the loaves in the oven for 30–35 minutes, or until they sound hollow when tapped on the base. Remove from the oven and leave to cool on a wire rack.

Homemade pitta bread

These can be a little challenging to make, but practice makes perfect with this recipe and the resulting pitta breads are delicious. Serve with any filling you like – great for a Saturday lunch with several filling options on the table to choose from.

Makes
12 pitta breads

500g (1lb 2oz) strong white bread flour, plus extra for dusting
2 tsp salt
7g sachet fast-action dried yeast
25g (1oz) unsalted butter, diced
1½ tsp black onion seeds
300ml (½ pint) warm water
vegetable oil, for oiling

1. Place the flour, salt, yeast, butter and onion seeds in the bowl of a food mixer with a dough hook. Mix on a low speed for 2–3 minutes, until the butter is incorporated into the flour. With the mixer still running slowly, pour in the warm water and mix until a dough forms. Continue to knead for 5 minutes, until smooth and elastic. (If you don't have a food mixer, mix together the flour, salt and yeast in a large mixing bowl. Add the butter and, using your fingertips, rub it in until the mixture resembles breadcrumbs. Stir in the onion seeds, then gradually add the warm water and lightly mix until a dough forms. Knead on a lightly floured surface for 10 minutes, until smooth and elastic.)

2. Transfer the dough to a lightly oiled bowl, cover loosely with clingfilm and put in a warm place to rise for about 1 hour, or until doubled in size. Preheat the oven to 240°C/fan 220°C/gas mark 9.

3. Punch the dough back down in size and divide into 12 pieces. Roll each piece of dough into a small ball, then flatten to form an oval 10 × 20cm (4 × 8in).

4. Dust each pitta bread lightly with flour, then place 2 at a time on a baking sheet and bake in the oven for 8–10 minutes. Keep the remaining unbaked pitta breads covered with a clean damp tea towel until ready to cook. After removing from the oven, wrap the cooked pitta breads in foil until ready to eat.

5. Serve the pitta breads either halved or split open and filled with your favourite things!

Soda bread

Homemade bread doesn't come easier than this, and it's a real winner on flavour too – it could even become your daily bread! It's especially delicious served warm with butter.

Makes 1 loaf

250g (9oz) wholemeal plain flour
250g (9oz) white self-raising flour
60g (2¼oz) porridge oats
1½ tsp salt
1 tsp bicarbonate of soda
25g (1oz) unsalted butter, diced
2 tbsp runny honey
500ml (18fl oz) buttermilk

1. Preheat the oven to 220°C/fan 200°C/gas mark 7.

2. Mix together all the dry ingredients in a large mixing bowl. Add the butter and, using your fingertips, rub it in until the mixture resembles breadcrumbs.

3. Mix together the honey and buttermilk, then add to the dry ingredients and mix together lightly until a dough forms.

4. Shape the dough into a round loaf about 20cm (8in) in diameter. Using a sharp knife, make a deep cross in the centre of the loaf, place on a baking sheet and bake in the oven for 30 minutes. Check that the loaf is baked by tapping on the base and listening for a hollow sound.

Cheesy bread rolls

This is a really quick, easy and tasty recipe – great for lunch boxes or dinner party bread baskets.

Makes 6 rolls

450g (1lb) plain wholemeal flour, plus extra for dusting (optional)
1 tsp runny honey
15g (½oz) fast-action dried yeast
1 tbsp salt
175g (6oz) mature Cheddar cheese, roughly grated, plus 50g (1¾oz)
  for sprinkling over the tops
275ml (9½fl oz) warm water
vegetable oil, for oiling
1 large beaten free-range egg, to glaze
cubes of butter, to serve

1. Place the flour, honey, yeast, salt and the 175g (6oz) Cheddar in the bowl of a food mixer with a dough hook. Mix briefly on a low speed until well combined. With the mixer still running slowly, pour in the warm water and mix until a dough forms. Continue to knead for about 5 minutes, until smooth and elastic. (If you don't have a food mixer, mix together the flour, honey, yeast, salt and Cheddar in a large mixing bowl. Add the warm water and mix until a soft dough forms. Knead the dough on a lightly floured surface for 10 minutes, until smooth and elastic.)

2. Transfer the dough to a lightly oiled large mixing bowl, cover loosely with clingfilm and put in a warm place to rise for about 45 minutes, or until doubled in size.

3. Punch the dough back down in size and divide into 6 pieces. Shape each piece of dough into a round roll and place on a baking sheet, allowing plenty of space between them. Brush the tops with beaten egg to glaze and sprinkle with remaining 50g (1¾oz) Cheddar. Cover lightly with a clean damp tea towel and leave in a warm place to prove for a further 30 minutes.

4. Preheat the oven to 220°C/fan 200°C/gas mark 7.

5. Bake the rolls in the oven for 40 minutes, or until they sound hollow when tapped on the base. Serve with cubes of butter for spreading.

Pesto & pancetta bread rolls

These rolls look so inviting, with their swirl of delicious homemade pesto inside, which also ensures that they remain nice and moist. They are fairly filling in themselves, so serve alongside a light supper or as a lunch with salad or soup.

Makes 8 rolls

140g (5oz) cubed pancetta, pan-fried

For the pesto
1 large bunch of flat leaf parsley, roughly chopped
leaves from 2 sprigs of rosemary, finely chopped
50g (1¾oz) pine nuts
2 garlic cloves, chopped
50g (1¾oz) Parmesan cheese, freshly grated
100ml (3½fl oz) olive oil
salt and black pepper

For the dough
500g (1lb 2oz) strong white bread flour, plus extra for dusting
7g sachet fast-action dried yeast
salt
100ml (3½fl oz) warm water
3 tbsp olive oil, plus extra for oiling
1 large beaten free-range egg, to glaze

1. Start by making the dough. Place the dry ingredients in the bowl of a food mixer with a dough hook. With the mixer on a low speed, pour in the warm water and olive oil and mix until a dough forms. Continue to knead for about 5 minutes, until smooth and elastic. (If you don't have a food mixer, place the dry ingredients in a large mixing bowl. Make a well in the centre, pour in the warm water and olive oil and mix well until a dough forms. Knead the dough on a lightly floured surface for 10 minutes, until smooth and elastic.)

2. Transfer the dough to a lightly oiled large mixing bowl, cover with a clean damp tea towel and put in a warm place to rise for about 45 minutes, or until doubled in size.

3. Meanwhile, make the pesto. Put the parsley, rosemary, pine nuts, garlic and Parmesan in a food processor and blitz. With the machine running, gradually add the olive oil until a smooth paste forms. Season to taste with salt and pepper.

4. Check the dough, and when it has doubled in size, punch it back down and knead on a lightly floured surface for 1 minute, then divide it in half. Roll out each half into an oblong about 1cm (½in) thick. Spoon over the pesto mix, spreading it evenly, then toss over the cooked pancetta cubes. With one of the short sides facing you, roll up each piece of dough into a sausage shape. Cut each roll into sections about 5cm (2in) wide.

5. Place the rolls on lightly oiled and parchment paper-lined baking sheets, leaving about 4cm (1½in) in between them. Cover lightly with a clean damp tea towel and leave in a warm place to prove for 30 minutes, or until well risen. Preheat the oven to 200°C/fan 180°C/gas mark 6.

6. Brush the rolls with beaten egg to glaze and bake in the oven for 15–20 minutes, until golden brown. Remove from the oven and immediately transfer to a wire rack to cool, so that the undersides don't overcook.

Baked vegetable & goats' cheese panini

Creating this recipe was daunting, as the kids love panini and are therefore harsh critics. But these passed with flying colours, even though they looked nothing like the end result before they were baked!

Makes 10 panini

For the panini dough
350g (12oz) strong white bread
   flour, plus extra if necessary and
   for dusting
150g (5½oz) plain flour
7g sachet fast-action dried yeast
1 tbsp salt
400ml (14fl oz) warm water
1 tbsp runny honey
3 tbsp olive oil, plus extra for oiling
1 large free-range egg, to glaze

For the filling
olive oil, for oiling and drizzling
2 courgettes, thickly sliced
1 red pepper and 1 yellow pepper,
   cored, deseeded and thinly sliced
1 aubergine, cut into 1cm (½in) cubes
1 red onion, thickly sliced
1 garlic clove, finely chopped
1 tbsp thyme leaves
salt and black pepper
100g (3½oz) goats' cheese, crumbled

For the pesto
3 handfuls of basil leaves
2 garlic cloves, chopped
2 tbsp freshly grated Parmesan
   cheese
squeeze of lemon juice
2 tbsp pine nuts
100ml (3½fl oz) olive oil
salt and black pepper

1. Start by making the dough. Place the dry ingredients in the bowl of a food mixer with a dough hook. With the mixer on a low speed, pour in the warm water, honey and olive oil and mix until a dough forms, adding a little more flour if it is too sticky. Continue to knead for about 5 minutes, until smooth and elastic. (If making by hand, place the dry ingredients in a large mixing bowl. Make a well in the centre, pour in the warm water, honey and olive oil and mix well until a dough forms. Knead the dough on a lightly floured surface for 10 minutes, until smooth and elastic.)

2. Transfer the dough to a lightly oiled large mixing bowl, cover with a clean damp tea towel and put in a warm place to rise for 40 minutes–1 hour, or until doubled in size.

3. Punch the dough back down in size, then return to the mixing bowl, cover again with the tea towel and put in a warm place to prove for 30 minutes, or until well risen. Preheat the oven to 190°C/fan 170°C/gas mark 5.

4. Meanwhile, begin preparing the filling. Lightly oil a roasting tin and add the courgettes, peppers, aubergine, red onion and garlic. Sprinkle over the thyme leaves, a few salt flakes and a grinding of black pepper. Drizzle over a little more oil and roast in the oven for 15 minutes. Remove from the oven and set aside for the moment. Turn the oven up to 200°C/fan 180°C/gas mark 6.

5. While the dough is proving and the vegetables are roasting, make the pesto. Place the basil leaves, garlic, Parmesan and lemon juice in a blender and blitz. Add the pine nuts and, with the machine running, gradually add the olive oil. Continue blitzing until smooth. Season with salt and pepper as necessary.

6. When the vegetables have finished roasting, stir 4 tbsp of the pesto into them, taking care not to crush them. Sprinkle over the goats' cheese.

7. Knock back the dough again and then divide into 10 pieces. Roll each piece out into a square about 1.5cm (⅝in) thick. Divide the filling mixture between the dough squares and place on one half of each square, leaving enough dough to fold over and encase the filling. Press down on the edge to seal each dough parcel. Place the panini on a lightly oiled baking sheet and leave to rest for 20 minutes.

8. Brush the panini with beaten egg and bake in the oven for 15–20 minutes, until lightly golden and bubbling.

Ham & cheese scones with sun-dried tomatoes

These keep really well in an airtight plastic container, so are ideal for making ahead and using for lunch or snack boxes, or just as a standby for a mid-afternoon weekend indulgence.

Makes 16 scones

750g (1lb 10oz) self-raising flour, plus extra for dusting
100g (3½oz) unsalted butter, cut into cubes
1 tsp salt
150g (5½oz) honey roast ham, cut into 5mm (¼in) cubes
150g (5½oz) mature Cheddar cheese, cut into 5mm (¼in) chunks
100g (3½oz) sun-dried tomatoes, finely chopped
500ml (18fl oz) double cream
150ml (¼ pint) milk

1. Sift the flour into a large bowl. Add the butter cubes and, using your fingertips, rub them in until the mixture resembles fine breadcrumbs. Stir through the salt. Add the ham, cheese and sun-dried tomatoes, mix through evenly, then make a well in the centre of the mixture. Pour in the cream and milk and, using a wooden spoon, lightly mix together into a wet dough – just gently combine the ingredients so that you don't mash the cheese and ham.

2. Wrap the scone dough in clingfilm and place in the refrigerator to chill for 20 minutes–1 hour.

3. Preheat the oven to 200°C/fan 180°C/gas mark 6. Place the dough on a lightly floured surface and cut into 16 pieces. Shape each piece of dough into a flattish triangle about 1.5cm (⅝in) thick and place on a baking sheet about 5cm (2in) apart.

4. Bake the scones in the oven for 25 minutes, or until lightly golden – the cheese bits should be bubbling and slightly crusty.

Easy quesadillas

These are fun for kids to make – say for a Saturday lunch when there's less pressure on time. You can even let them come up with their own ideas of what would be a good filling!

Serves 4

8 × 20cm (8in) flour tortillas
olive oil, for brushing
120g (4¼oz) tub fresh ready-made basil pesto
4 tbsp grated fontina cheese
8 slices of salami, cut into strips
20 sun-dried tomatoes, roughly sliced

1. Preheat the oven to 200°C/fan 180°C/gas mark 6.

2. Lightly brush the tortillas with olive oil and place 4, oiled side down, on a baking sheet. Spread 1 tbsp of the pesto over the top of each tortilla on the baking sheet, then sprinkle 1 tbsp of the fontina over the pesto.

3. Arrange the salami strips and the sun-dried tomato slices on top of the pesto and cheese, then cover each tortilla with another tortilla, oiled side up.

4. Bake in the oven for 8–10 minutes, until the tops of the tortillas are nicely golden and the filling bubbling. Remove from the oven and transfer to a chopping board. Cut into wedges – but take care, as the cheese in the centre will be very hot.

Easter,
Hallowe'en &
Christmas

Chocolate peppermint cookies

This is the homemade gift that's guaranteed to make your child teacher's pet at Christmas time! Place three or four of the cookies in a cellophane bag and finish off with a pretty ribbon tied in a bow.

Makes
24 cookies

For the cookie dough
70g (2½oz) unsalted butter, softened, plus extra for greasing
90g (3¼oz) granulated sugar
2 large free-range eggs, beaten
1 tsp peppermint extract
180g (6¼oz) plain flour, plus extra for dusting
60g (2¼oz) cocoa powder
½ tsp baking powder

For the coating
200g (7oz) white chocolate, roughly chopped
200g (7oz) plain dark chocolate (70% cocoa solids), roughly chopped
20 boiled sweets, crushed

1. For the cookie dough, beat together the butter and sugar using a food mixer with a paddle attachment, or with a wooden spoon in a large mixing bowl, until pale and fluffy. Add the eggs a little at a time, beating after each addition, then the peppermint extract. Sift together the flour, cocoa and baking powder, then gradually fold into the cookie mixture in stages with a large metal spoon, keeping as much air in the mixture as you can, until it is all incorporated and a dough forms.

2. Wrap the cookie dough in clingfilm and place in the refrigerator to chill for 1 hour. Lightly grease 2 baking sheets and line with parchment paper.

3. Roll out the cookie dough on a lightly floured surface until about 1cm (½in) thick. Using a selection of cutters, each measuring about 6cm (2½in), cut out shapes and place on the prepared baking sheets leaving a space of 4cm (1½in) between each cookie. Cover loosely with clingfilm and leave in the refrigerator for 15 minutes or so to rest the dough and prevent the cookies from spreading too much when you bake them. Preheat the oven to 200°C/fan 180°C/gas mark 6.

4. Bake the cookies in the oven for 10–12 minutes, until firm to the touch. Remove from the oven and immediately transfer to a wire rack to cool completely. Place a clean sheet of parchment paper on each baking sheet.

5. While the cookies are cooling, melt the white and plain dark chocolate separately, each in a heatproof mixing bowl set over a saucepan of gently simmering water, so that the base of the bowl doesn't touch the water. Once the chocolates have begun to melt, stir briskly until smooth.

6. Meanwhile, place the boiled sweets in a double layer of plastic bags and, using a rolling pin, crush them to a fine powder (but it is OK to leave some slightly larger pieces). Tip into a bowl.

7. Using a pair of tongs, take each cooled cookie one at a time and dip either in the melted white or plain dark chocolate, turning it over to make sure that it is evenly coated. Lay on the parchment-lined baking sheets to harden. While the chocolate is still molten, sprinkle over the crushed boiled sweets to allow them to sink into the coating a little.

Honey-spice nuts

Homemade snacks make a great addition to the indulgence that we all partake in at special times of year, and this sweet yet spicy festive treat is suitably simple and satisfying.

Serves 4–6

125ml (4fl oz) runny honey
2 tsp salt flakes
1 tsp cracked black pepper
¼ tsp ground allspice
¼ tsp cayenne pepper
½ tsp chilli powder
½ tsp ground cumin
500g (1lb 2 oz) mixed nuts, such as
    cashew nuts, almonds, pecan nuts,
    hazelnuts and walnuts
2 tbsp soft dark brown sugar

1. Preheat the oven to 200°C/fan 180°C/gas mark 6. Line a baking sheet with parchment paper.

2. Put all the ingredients, except the sugar, in a large mixing bowl and stir together well, making sure that you coat all the nuts in the mixture.

3. Scatter the nuts over the lined baking sheet and bake in the oven for 15 minutes. Remove from the oven and sprinkle over the sugar. Return to the oven for a further 5 minutes.

4. Remove the nuts from the oven and leave to cool before serving.

Cranberry & orange hot cross buns

I love basic hot cross buns, but this recipe takes them to a whole new level with the combination of these two fab flavours. Simply serve warm with butter.

Makes 12 buns

100ml (3½fl oz) warm water, plus extra if necessary
7g sachet fast-action dried yeast
450g (1lb) plain flour, plus extra if necessary and for dusting
½ tsp ground cinnamon
1½ tsp mixed spice
50g (1¾oz) butter, cut into small cubes, plus extra for greasing
finely grated zest of 2 unwaxed oranges
80g (2¾oz) dried cranberries
100ml (3½fl oz) warm milk
1 large free range egg, beaten, plus extra to attach the crosses and to glaze
vegetable oil, for oiling
100g (3½oz) ready-made shortcrust pastry

For the glaze
1 tbsp hot water
1 tbsp smooth orange marmalade
1 tbsp soft dark brown sugar

1. Put the warm water in a mixing bowl, add the yeast and stir together, then leave the mixture for about 30 minutes, until it starts to froth.

2. Meanwhile, place the flour, cinnamon and mixed spice in a large mixing bowl and add the butter cubes. Using your fingertips, rub the butter in until the mixture resembles breadcrumbs.

3. At this stage, if you have a food mixer you can mix all the ingredients together with a dough hook; otherwise, continue with the mixing bowl and a wooden spoon. Make a well in the centre and tip in the yeast mixture. Add the orange zest and cranberries, and mix well until distributed throughout. Add the warm milk and egg, and continue mixing until the mixture comes together into a dough. If the dough is too sticky, add a little more flour, or alternatively add a touch more warm water if the dough is too firm. You should be able to handle the dough without it sticking too much to your hands. Knead the dough for 5 minutes in the food mixer, or 10 minutes by hand on a lightly floured surface, until smooth and elastic.

4. Place the dough in a lightly oiled mixing bowl, cover with a clean damp tea towel and leave in a warm place to rise for about 1 hour, or until doubled in size.

5. Punch the dough back down in size. Divide into 12 even-sized pieces and place them on a lightly greased baking sheet lined with parchment paper – bear in mind that they will double in size again, so leave plenty of space between them. Cover again with the tea towel and leave in a warm place for about 1 hour, or until doubled in size. Preheat the oven to 220°C/fan 200°C/gas mark 7.

6. To make the crosses, roll out the shortcrust pastry on a lightly floured surface until about 3mm (⅛in) thick and cut out thin pastry strips. Brush the risen buns with beaten egg, lay on the pastry crosses and brush once again with the egg.

7. Bake in the oven for 15–20 minutes, until they are lovely and golden and sound hollow if you tap them underneath.

8. Meanwhile, place the ingredients for the glaze in a small saucepan and heat until the sugar has dissolved and the marmalade has loosened. As soon as the buns are ready, remove from the oven, paint on the glaze and leave to cool slightly before tucking in.

Basic cookies

I use this very simple biscuit recipe when I want to make shapes and ice them for Christmas, Hallowe'en or Easter. All you need do is adjust the icing colour or cookie cutter to suit the season.

Makes approximately 22 large cookies

For the cookie dough
200g (7oz) unsalted butter, softened, plus extra for greasing
100g (3½oz) granulated sugar
1 tsp finely grated unwaxed lemon zest
1 large free-range egg, beaten
½ tsp vanilla extract
300g (10½oz) plain flour, sifted, plus extra for dusting

For the glacé icing
200g (7oz) icing sugar, sifted
3 tbsp water
food colouring of your choice
sprinkle decorations of your choice

1. Beat together the butter, sugar and lemon zest using a food mixer with a paddle attachment, or with a wooden spoon in a large mixing bowl, until pale and fluffy. Add the egg and vanilla extract a little at a time, beating after each addition, then gradually fold in the flour with a large metal spoon until it is all incorporated and a dough forms.

2. Wrap the cookie dough in clingfilm and place in the refrigerator to chill for up to 1 hour. Preheat the oven to 200°C/fan 180°C/gas mark 6. Lightly grease 2 baking sheets and line with parchment paper.

3. Remove the dough from the refrigerator and leave until soft enough to roll out – this may take 5 minutes. Roll out on a lightly floured surface to about 5mm (¼in) thick and cut out your chosen shapes, re-rolling any offcuts. Lay the cookies on the prepared baking sheets, leaving a space of 4cm (1½in) between each cookie, and immediately bake in the oven for 12–15 minutes, until lightly golden.

4. Remove the cookies from the oven and transfer to a wire rack. Leave to cool completely.

5. To make the glacé icing, place the icing sugar in a large mixing bowl. Add the water and mix well until smooth. Beat in a few drops of food colouring of your choice. Decorate the cooled cookies by carefully spreading over the glacé icing and topping with sprinkles.

Snowball cupcakes

These cupcakes are really fun to make as well as glorious to bite into, with their centres scooped out and filled with marshmallow that will gently melt with the heat of the sponge.

Makes 12 cupcakes

200g (7oz) unsalted butter, softened
200g (7oz) caster sugar
4 large free-range eggs, beaten
170g (6oz) plain flour
30g (1oz) cocoa powder
12 white marshmallows

For the white chocolate frosting
125g (4½oz) white chocolate
125ml (4fl oz) double cream

To decorate
30g (1oz) desiccated coconut
25g (1oz) edible silver balls
white chocolate shavings

1. Preheat the oven to 200°C/fan 180°C/gas mark 6. Line a 12-hole cupcake tin with cupcake cases.

2. Beat together the butter and the sugar using a food mixer with a paddle attachment, or with a wooden spoon in a large mixing bowl, until pale and fluffy. Add the eggs a little at a time, beating after each addition, then sift in the flour and cocoa powder and fold in with a large metal spoon until well mixed.

3. Divide the sponge mixture between the cupcake cases, filling them around half full. Bake in the oven for about 15 minutes, until the cupcakes spring back to the touch of a fingertip.

4. Meanwhile, slice about 5mm (¼in) off the bottom of each marshmallow.

5. Remove the cupcakes from the oven. While the cakes are still hot, take a sharp knife and gently cut a hollow in the centre of each cake, leaving a 5mm (¼in) border around the outside. Place a trimmed marshmallow in each hollow so that it sits flush with the surface of the cupcake – they will slightly melt into the cavities. Leave the cakes to cool in the tin.

6. Meanwhile, make the white chocolate frosting. Chop the white chocolate into small chunks and place in a heatproof bowl set over a saucepan of gently simmering water, making sure that the base doesn't touch the water. Stir to help the chocolate melt and become a smooth, glossy liquid. Whip the cream until stiff, then fold into the melted white chocolate. Set aside to cool.

7. When the cupcakes and frosting are completely cool, spread the frosting generously over the tops of the cakes, sprinkle over the coconut and decorate with the silver balls and white chocolate shavings.

spiced orange & cranberry mince pies

Mince pies are such a Christmas classic, but the filling in these is refreshingly light and clean-tasting, so you don't feel that you have over-indulged – even if you eat a couple!

Makes
18 mince pies

For the pastry
350g (12oz) plain flour, plus extra for dusting
225g (8oz) unsalted butter, chilled and cut into cubes
100g (3½oz) caster sugar
pinch of salt
2 tsp finely grated unwaxed orange zest
few drops of vanilla extract
1 large beaten free-range egg, to glaze
sifted icing sugar, for dusting

For the filling
350g (12oz) mincemeat
2 tsp finely grated unwaxed orange zest
30g (1oz) dried cranberries
15g (½oz) flaked almonds
2 tsp brandy
pinch of chilli flakes

1. Start by making the pastry. Sift the flour into a large mixing bowl and add the butter cubes. Using your fingertips, rub the butter in until the mixture resembles fine breadcrumbs. Mix in the sugar, salt, orange zest and vanilla extract, and combine the pastry into a ball. Work together using your hands, as it will be fairly firm. Wrap the dough in clingfilm and place in the refrigerator to chill for 30 minutes.

2. While the pastry is chilling, mix together all the filling ingredients in a large mixing bowl. Preheat the oven to 220°C/fan 200°C/gas mark 7.

3. Roll out the pastry dough on a lightly floured surface until about 5mm (¼in) thick. Using a 7cm (2¾in) round cutter, cut out 18 circles and use to line 18 holes of two 12-hole nonstick cupcake tins. Spoon an equal quantity of the filling into each pastry case.

4. From the remaining pastry, cut out different shapes for the lids, such as stars or bells, and use to cover the pies, re-rolling any offcuts. Press gently on top to seal.

5. Brush the tops of the pies with beaten egg to glaze. Bake in the oven for 20–25 minutes, until golden brown. Leave to cool in the tin for a few minutes before transferring to a wire rack. To serve, dust lightly with icing sugar.

Triple cheese straws with mustard & thyme

These sit fantastically well in the centre of the table when you are entertaining. They're light and delicious but very moreish, so it's just as well that the recipe makes plenty!

Makes approximately 20 straws

125g (4½oz) butter, chilled and cut into cubes, plus extra for greasing
75g (2¾oz) wholemeal plain flour
60g (2¼oz) white plain flour, plus extra for dusting
1 large free-range egg, separated
40g (1½oz) mature Cheddar cheese, grated
30g (1oz) Parmesan cheese, freshly grated
30g (1oz) Red Leicester cheese, grated
1 tsp wholegrain mustard
2 tsp thyme leaves
pinch of salt
poppy or sesame seeds, for sprinkling

1. Preheat the oven to 220°C/fan 200°C/gas mark 7. Lightly grease a baking sheet and line with parchment paper.

2. Start by sifting and mixing the flours together in a large mixing bowl. Add the butter cubes and, using your fingertips, rub them in until the mixture resembles fine breadcrumbs. Lightly beat the egg yolk and stir into the mixture with all the cheeses, the mustard, thyme leaves and salt. Mix well until a dough forms. Cover loosely with clingfilm and place in the refrigerator to chill for at least 45 minutes.

3. Turn the dough out on to a lightly floured surface and roll out until about 1cm (½in) thick. Cut out your cheese straws, making them any size you wish, but I usually go for 1.5cm (⅝in) wide by 15cm (6in) long. Lightly beat the egg white, then brush over the straws. Sprinkle with poppy or sesame seeds and gently push them into the pastry.

4. Place the cheese straws on the prepared baking sheet and bake in the oven for 10–12 minutes, or until golden brown. Remove from the oven and immediately slide the straws on to a wire rack to cool.

Whole baked Camembert

Serves 4 as a starter

1 large Camembert in its wooden case
1 small garlic clove, cut into thin slivers
few sprigs of rosemary
salt and black pepper

For dipping
celery sticks, walnuts and raisins

This is the simplest yet most delicious and indulgent savoury treat. Brie is just as wonderful prepared in this way. As an alternative to serving with the dipping treats, spread on to toasted slices of bread, adding a teaspoon of homemade Tomato & Chilli Jam (see page 153) to each slice.

1. Preheat the oven to 220°C/fan 200°C/gas mark 7.

2. Simply remove the lid of the Camembert, unwrap the cheese and place back in the box. Make a few incisions in the cheese and insert the garlic slivers and rosemary sprigs. Sprinkle with salt and pepper and place on a baking sheet.

3. Bake in the oven for 15 minutes, or until you can see that the cheese is soft and bubbling under the crust.

4. Serve immediately with the dipping treats listed.

Chocolate log with orange & raspberry

I think of this chocolate Swiss roll as a Christmas dessert, although the raspberries would at first appear to contradict that, as they are a summer fruit. However, the frozen berries you can buy are delicious.

Serves 6-8

For the sponge
butter, for greasing
4 large free-range eggs, at room temperature
100g (3½oz) caster sugar, plus 1 tbsp for sprinkling
90g (3¼oz) plain flour
20g (¾oz) cocoa powder

For the filling
150ml (¼ pint) whipping cream
finely grated zest and juice of 1 unwaxed orange
1 tsp vanilla extract
25g (1oz) icing sugar, sifted, plus extra if necessary
50ml (2fl oz) mascarpone cheese
100g (3½oz) punnet raspberries, crushed

For the frosting
175g (6oz) plain dark chocolate (70% cocoa solids), roughly chopped
175g (6oz) unsalted butter, softened
175g (6oz) icing sugar, sifted, plus extra for dusting
few drops of vanilla extract

1. Preheat the oven to 200°C/fan 180°C/gas mark 6. Lightly grease a 25 × 35cm (10 × 14in) Swiss roll tin or large baking tin and line with parchment paper, making sure that you have an extra 5cm (2in) of paper on all sides to help you turn out the cooked sponge.

2. For the sponge, whisk together the eggs and sugar in a large mixing bowl with an electric whisk or food mixer until thick, pale and creamy, and the whisk leaves a trail when you lift it out of the mixture.

3. Sift together the flour and cocoa and mix well. Gradually fold into the egg mixture with a large metal spoon in stages, taking care to keep as much of the air in the mixture as possible, until all the flour mixture is incorporated.

4. Carefully turn the sponge mixture into the prepared tin, then use a palette knife to gently spread it into the corners and smooth off the top. Bake in the oven for 10-12 minutes, until the sponge is lightly golden and springs back to the touch of a fingertip.

5. Remove the sponge from the oven and set aside for a moment. Cut a sheet of parchment paper slightly larger in size than the tin, lay it on the work surface and sprinkle it evenly with the remaining 1 tbsp caster sugar. Quickly but carefully turn the sponge out face down on the sugar layer, then gently peel away the lining paper. Leave to cool completely.

6. Now make the filling. Put the cream in a large, clean mixing bowl along with the orange zest and juice, vanilla extract and icing sugar, and whisk until soft peaks form. Fold in the mascarpone, then toss in the crushed raspberries. Check the sweetness, adding more icing sugar if necessary, then spread evenly over the sponge, leaving a 2cm (¾in) border of clear sponge at either side.

7. With one of the short ends of the sponge facing you, use the parchment paper to help you carefully roll it up into a neat log, finishing with the seam on the underside.

8. To make the frosting, melt the chocolate in a heatproof mixing bowl set over a saucepan of gently simmering water, making sure that the base doesn't touch the water. Meanwhile, put the butter, icing sugar and vanilla extract in a large mixing bowl and use a hand whisk or electric whisk to beat together until pale and fluffy. Add the melted chocolate and whisk well to combine.

9. Spread the frosting over the chocolate log, using a palette knife or fork to create the desired finish – work quickly, as the frosting will soon set.

Index

Acknowledgements

To Olly, the most amazing sister – thank you x

It takes so many people to put together a book like this – huge amounts of dedication, patience, time and, of course, lots of hair-pulling in frustration – but with laughter thrown into the mix, too. It is impossible to know where to start in thanking everybody so, in no particular order...

As always, a massive thank you to Gordon, Megan, Jack, Holly and Tilly for putting up with chaos in the kitchen at times and giving honest opinions on all the dishes I presented you with!

Thank you to Tucker for running out to get obscure ingredients and helping to carry around all the shopping; Yolly for your help with the endless washing up; Karen, Lisa and Chris for many enjoyable shoots and testing sessions – they're always so much fun and we never seem to stop eating or laughing!

Thanks to Chris Terry for the most amazing shoots – it never felt like work as I just cooked and talked and somehow we got all the shots done (with little tweaks for presentation from Karen along the way...). Thank you also to Danny.

Becca, as always it is so lovely to work with you. You have had endless patience with me on this book – chasing text and listening to the concerns I have had – and as usual you are so calm and reassuring, and we got there eventually. I am sure there were many times you questioned it, but we did it!

Pene, thank you for making everything look so gorgeous – and for your constant calming influence on us all.

Leanne, thanks for putting everything together so beautifully.

And lastly, to all those people behind the scenes who make it possible for my book to come together – thank you.

First published in Great Britain in 2011 by Mitchell Beazley,
an imprint of Octopus Publishing Group Limited, Endeavour House,
189 Shaftesbury Avenue, London, WC2H 8JY
www.octopusbooks.co.uk

An Hachette UK Company
www.hachette.co.uk

Copyright © Octopus Publishing Group Ltd 2011
Text copyright © Tana Ramsay 2011
Photography copyright © Chris Terry 2011

ISBN: 978 1 84533 548 9

A CIP record for this book is available from the British Library.

Printed and bound in China

Editorial Director | Tracey Smith

Commissioning Editor | Becca Spry

Senior Editor | Leanne Bryan

Art Director and Designer | Pene Parker

Copy-editor | Jo Richardson

Photographer | Chris Terry

Home Economists | Karen Taylor, Lisa Harrison, Chris Taylor

Stylist | Sarah O'Keefe

Proofreader | Jo Murray

Indexer | Isobel McLean

Production Manager | Peter Hunt